RECIPES FOR LIFE

Beautiful Food and Words to Live By

Ohén:ton Karihwatéhkwen

Words Before All Else

RECIPES FOR LIFE

Beautiful Food and Words to Live By

Madeleine Marentette

Grail Springs Retreat
Centre for Wellbeing

First published 2015 by

M & M Productions
2004 Bay Lake Road
Bancroft, ON
K0L 1C0

www.grailsprings.com

Copyright © 2015 Madeleine Marentette

Library and Archives Canada Cataloguing in Publication

Marentette, Madeleine   Grail Springs / Madeleine Marentette

Includes index ISBN 992153113-1

www.grailsprings.com

Design and composition by Madeleine Marentette and Marsha Pace

Printed in Canada by Transcontinental

Main cover photographs: Nanne Springer
Interior photographs: Nanne Springer
                               John Parson
                               Madeleine Marentette
                               Michael Moon

For specific details on a photograph or contact information for any of the above photographers, please email reservations@grailsprings.com.

Dedicated to
the Grail Springs Community

Table of Contents

Foreword

Gratitude. This is the word that comes to mind when I think about Grail Springs. Like a giddy young girl upon the mention of her teenage crush, my stomach turns to butterflies when I ponder a possible return. My affair with the place began before it became Grail Springs. Bride's Gate was what it was called then, when I had my first romantic rendezvous with my honey Peter. Even then, while dining on chicken and wine, the place had a healing effect. Throughout the years Madeleine has transformed Grail Springs into a world famous healing retreat. She travels the globe and brings back new treatments and inspirations that assist in the healing process.

My family gets jealous of my love affair with Grail Springs. Dad often grumbles, "What is this Grail place you keep escaping to?" Someday I might bring him to this place...maybe. Only maybe, because I pause when I consider sharing this oasis. In short it is a soulful refueling station. A place for spiritual re-grounding built on quartz crystal land. The offerings of Grail Springs include: numerous healing modalities; a labyrinth and tepees; hiking trails and horses; beautifully appointed rooms (some with a fireplace and balcony overlooking a serene lake), plus so much more. A day begins with Grail's Morning Mantra, meditation and yoga, and ends with inspirational speakers or events. Oh, and did I mention that the vegetarian food is divine? Food that is creative, nourishing, wholesome and worthy of this cookbook.

All that and more helps to invoke a celebration of life and nature, instilling faith that there is a magical place where it is safe to blossom within. That place is Grail Springs.

by Leah Pinsent, Actress

King Lear late at night on the cliffs

asks the blind Earl of Gloucester

"How do you see the world?"

And the blind man of Gloucester replies

"I see it feelingly."

Introduction

Recipes for Life: Beautiful Food and Words to Live By

North America is experiencing the largest aging population in history. People are highly motivated to take purpose-driven wellness getaways instead of opting for the all-you-can-eat-and-drink beach resort vacations. Many are seeking out holistic-focused resorts, yoga retreats, healing hotels and wellness centres around the world. This zest for knowledge and longevity will continue to grow as the general population is exposed to ongoing physical, mental and emotional challenges resulting from high productivity demands in the workplace, food processing, genetically modified foods, animal factory farming, wireless technology and pollution. Each new generation encounters their own unique problems. It is up to us to educate and empower ourselves by engaging in the political process, voting for what is right and voting against what is not. It is up to us to put our consumer dollars to the vote by purchasing ethically produced products and refusing to buy those that are not. This is how we message governments and large corporations to bend towards what is right for our children, our planet and for us. It starts with the collective community, aware and empowered as a whole.

It is not such a big leap to see and feel that society functions as a single mass organism. Individually we contribute to a bigger wave, moving together energetically in patterns as one great big ocean, reacting to environmental, social, economic and political currents. We see this in business all the time. There are ebbs and flows in consumer spending. And paradigm shifts can happen when there is passionate leadership, examples set, media support, and social messaging campaigns. At one time, people didn't recycle. Attitudes toward cigarette smoking and littering have changed. As a child growing up in Ontario, I clearly remember the garbage that lined the highways.

Today, no one would even think to throw a coffee cup out the window. As this book goes to print the anti-texting while driving campaign is taking hold on the mass consciousness and will soon find people getting used to checking emails or making their calls prior to getting in the car. Mass shifts can happen. It simply takes a change of perspective supported by good leadership.

Philip Wollen, an Australian philanthropist (and former vice-president of Citibank), is widely known for his views and passion to end animal factory farming. At a debate in Melbourne, Australia, which landed him thousands of views on YouTube, he opened with these words:

> *"King Lear late at night on the cliffs asks the blind*
> *Earl of Gloucester, 'How do you see the world?'*
> *And the blind man of Gloucester replies, 'I see it feelingly'.*

There is undeniable group sensitivity to the condition of the world today. Many of us experience a feeling of unsteadiness, insecurity and even fear about the way in which humanity as a whole is proceeding into the future. We watch the news, shake our heads, and wonder what the world is coming to. And then we may make an agreement with ourselves to turn off the news, resolve there is nothing we can do personally to help, and then get on with our day. However in our own hearts and consciences an energy pulsates with the undeniable awareness that there is disharmony and violence occurring everyday amongst our collective humanity, violence against each other, the animal kingdom and the planet. To negate the feeling of knowing this, and what makes us uncomfortable, and to not doing anything about it is at the demise of our own personal future and the future of all of us.

Grail Springs Retreat Centre for Wellbeing, located in Bancroft, Ontario, Canada, has been dedicated to the wellbeing of people, animals and the planet for over two decades. In order for Grail Springs to be in alignment with my own values, including my work with animal welfare rights, I decided to make what was considered by advisors a risky business decision in 2008. I eliminated meat altogether from the table. Taking a stand for animal welfare came with lots of unforeseen benefits. The move was aligned with the acid/alkaline approach to diet which many doctors and naturopaths support today. Health practitioners understand the significance of maintaining a pH balanced body in order to combat disease and keep our bio-energy charged.

We at Grail Springs are helping our guests to live long and happy lives, while we no longer contribute to big corporate factory farms. Grail Springs thrives and guests enjoy the lovingly prepared, delicious vegetarian food.

Grail Springs has been blessed to have friends and guests visit from all over the world. The Grail Springs community is comprised of caring staff and numerous teachers, healers, spiritual leaders of all faiths, activists, authors, musicians and transformational leaders. Within the Grail Springs community there is a common interest ~ to make the world and ourselves better for all.

This book is a compilation of recipes for life ~ beautiful food and words of wisdom from our community, accompanied by photos of Grail Springs Retreat Centre for Wellbeing. I hope the following pages offer you inspiration and opportunity for many wonderful meals gathered with friends and loved ones. Food is a universal language, inspiring us to remember what we truly value in life - being connected through love and shared values. May each of us follow our true conscience ~ the divinely given compass that always leads us to feel our way through life, feel our way to the truth, beauty and the harmony we seek for all.

~ Madeleine Marentette

I surrendered to her gentle persuasion.
I heard a soft, familiar voice.
"Follow me" she said...

Come to the Table

I surrendered to her gentle persuasion. I heard a soft, familiar voice, "Follow me" she said…

I could see nothing else but a graceful hand reaching out and taking mine. She led me up a dimly lit staircase from what appeared to be a shadowy, but familiar cellar. In the darkness I caught a glimpse of her petite and youthful feet with wisps of her gown catching the light from above, lavender blue and translucent.

As we reached a landing, I realized this home was known to me from years past, but it appeared all in reverse and not at all how I had left it. The hazardous electrical wires and water lines that were once hanging from the ceiling were now sealed up behind finished walls, smooth and painted. The dust, old plaster, debris, scaffolding and scattered tools were gone. Someone had finished the task that I had started two decades ago, abandoned at a time when life was challenging me in every possible way. I was now seeing the restoration of my first home; symbolic of my long journey in forgiveness, healing and coming to peace; my internal self-restoration.

The room was lit for only a moment, enough for me to see that all was restored and pristine. I felt this as a gift of confirmation, that all was finally complete to the core of my soul. Carrying a deep sense of gratitude, I was now being led to the middle of the room where a substantial medieval dining table appeared with six wooden throne-like chairs, modest in their simplicity.

But there was nothing else earthly about this place. The table settings were of glistening silver, chalices of clear cut crystal and dishes of white porcelain. Each of the six plates was larger than normal, the size of chargers, and became illuminated before my eyes while all else faded to black. Amber cone-shaped beams of light descended from above and encircled each plate. Unable to see the source, these beams of lights were made of glistening strings of pearl-like beads, moving in a continuous downward motion. I was transfixed. My host let go of my hand and I broke my gaze. She pulled out a chair and beckoned me to have a seat at this heavenly table. I sat down. She disappeared.

My focus went to my plate. Never had I seen anything so white, so pure in this world, and I acknowledged what I was seeing was not of this earth. I reached in through the amber beads, compelled to touch this ring of illumination. I watched in slow motion as the strings of light broke and spilled. As the beads rolled off the back of my hand they reconnected themselves underneath my palm, liquid-like, the way mercury beads break away and comes back to itself. The strings effortlessly restored themselves to perfect form. A thought entered my consciousness: we are all born to come back to ourselves.

In an immense state of wonderment and reverence, I looked up at the other five plates and silently wondered, "Who will join me at this heavenly table?"...

By now you know this is a dream, full of metaphor and meaning. I had this dream in 2010 when I was contemplating another recipe book collection for Grail Springs.

The residual energy of the dream lasted for several weeks, even months. Just thinking of it now moves me to that same sense of wonderment. The dream overall told me one thing: this book was going to be a creation from the heart and one of divine inspiration; to help others restore their own health, their love for life, reconnect with self and the experience of oneness will all things. For all is connected.

The world is ever-changing. We at Grail Springs envision a kinder, gentler society that accepts our differences and excels in compassion for others, including our animal population and the earth on which we all depend. This book is divinely inspired for food lovers, animal lovers, earth lovers, and lovers of Life itself. Won't you join us, and take a seat at our heavenly table of divine design?

May your cup overflow with many blessings.

~ Madeleine Marentette

The Grail Mantra: Gratitude, Humilty, Grace, Reverence

Adding daily movement to your life boosts your

electro-immune system, charges your energy field,

energizes your soul,

and helps raise your life to a higher vibration.

Doing a little more of what you love each day

helps you love your life a little more.

~ David Price Francis, Author, Founder of Energy Worlds

BEGINNINGS

Smoothies & Shakes

Coconut Water Dragon

1½ cups pre-brewed lemongrass tea, cooled

½ cup coconut water or plain water

¼ cup shredded coconut

1 to 2 teaspoons sprouted chia seeds

1 teaspoon acai powder

2 tablespoons black sesame seeds

1 teaspoon vanilla powder

1 tablespoon coconut oil

1 to 2 teaspoons chlorella powder or spirulina powder

Preparation

Add all ingredients and turn blender on low until the mixture is moving smoothly. Blend well on medium for approximately 1 minute.

Serves 2

Amazon Mecca Smoothie

2 cups of your favourite brewed herbal tea, cooled

4 dried apricots or juice from one orange

1 teaspoon maqui berry powder

½ cup blueberries, or 2 teaspoons of blueberry powder

1 teaspoon camu camu berry powder

1½ tablespoons sprouted chia powder or flax powder

1 teaspoon acai berry powder

2 tablespoons coconut oil

2 teaspoons honey

1 cup ice cubes

Preparation

Add all ingredients except ice cubes and turn blender on low until the mixture is moving smoothly. Add ice cubes. Blend well on high for approximately 1 minute.

Serves 2

It's important to understand nature and look at her through the eyes of a child, and that's through innocence and imagination; to want to understand nature rather than eliminate or control her. We have to make a stand here as individuals, make a commitment to give back and support Mother Earth.

~ Alan Reed, Geomancer

Bee-utiful Berry Smoothie

3 cups of almond milk
¼ cup flax seed, ground to a fine meal
1 teaspoon cinnamon
½ cup berries: blueberries, blackberries, cherries, or raspberries
1 avocado
1 heaping teaspoon super greens powder
3 heaping tablespoons fresh bee pollen
3 tablespoons flax seed oil
1 tablespoon raw, organic honey
Pinch of Himalayan salt

Preparation

Grind the flax seeds along with cinnamon in a coffee grinder and set
aside. Pour almond milk into blender.
Add all other ingredients and turn blender on low until the mixture is
moving smoothly.
Blend well on high for 1 minute or until desired consistency.

Serves 2

Chia and Banana Cacao Smoothie

½ banana

2 tablespoons raw cacao powder

1 tablespoon sprouted chia seeds

½ teaspoon spirulina or chlorella powder

½ to 1 teaspoon vanilla powder

1 or 2 dashes of cinnamon

2 cups almond milk

Maple syrup or stevia to taste

Preparation

Add all ingredients and turn blender on low until the mixture is moving smoothly. Blend well on medium for approximately 1 minute.

Serves 2

Go Goji

½ cup goji berries

½ cup any berries in season

¼ cup raw almonds

2 cups almond milk

2 tablespoons raw cacao or chocolate protein powder

1 or 2 dashes of cinnamon

1 tablespoon honey

1 cup ice cubes

Preparation

Place all ingredients in a blender except ice cubes and blend until smooth. Adjust cocoa powder and cinnamon to taste. Add ice cubes and blend on high speed for a thicker smoothie.

Serves 2

The ingredients for a happy life are simple and true:
Mix lots of gratitude and love to begin the brew.
Add compassion, flexibility and an open mind to the mixture,
then stir in forgiveness to get the right texture.
Sprinkle on top some laughter and play,
and enjoy the final product generously each day!

~ Evita Ochel, Consciousness Expansion Teacher

Love Me Tender Shake

2 cups almond milk

½ cup strawberries

¼ cup almonds

1 tablespoon chia powder

1 tablespoon cacao nibs (optional)

2 or 3 tablespoons raw cacao powder

Pinch of cinnamon

1 teaspoon vanilla powder

1 tablespoon honey

Preparation

Add all ingredients and turn blender on low until the mixture is moving smoothly. Blend well on medium for approximately 1 minute.

Serves 2

Chia seeds are an excellent source of fibre, protein, antioxidants and they are gluten free.

Cinnamon contains anti-inflammatory compounds that can be useful in reducing pain and inflammation associated with arthritis.

Holy Stress Buster

2 cups pre-brewed holy basil tea, cooled

½ cup frozen blueberries or 1 teaspoon blueberry powder

1½ teaspoon chia or flax powder

1 teaspoon maqui powder

1 teaspoon maca X-6 powder

2 teaspoons ashwagandha powder

1 teaspoon camu camu powder

¼ teaspoon stevia powder or maple syrup to taste

Preparation

Add all ingredients and turn blender on low until the mixture is moving smoothly. Blend well on medium for approximately 1 minute.

Serves 2

Chai and Cashew Latte Smoothie to Live for!

3 pitted dates

1 ½ cups unsweetened cashew milk

½ teaspoon ground ginger

1 teaspoon cinnamon

½ teaspoon ground cardamom

½ teaspoon ground nutmeg

½ teaspoon ground clove

1 teaspoon super greens powder

1 tablespoon raw protein powder

Preparation

Place all ingredients in a blender and blend until smooth.
Adjust spices to taste and add ice for a thicker smoothie.

Serves 2

Blueberry and Maple Syrup Smoothie

1 cup ice

1 teaspoon almond extract

1 teaspoon vanilla extract

2 tablespoons maple syrup

1 cup frozen blueberries

1 cup almond milk

2 tablespoon raw ground almonds

1 teaspoon super greens powder

1 tablespoon raw protein powder

Preparation

Place all ingredients in a blender, blend and serve.

Maple syrup is a natural sweetener with the same classes of anti-oxident compounds that are found in berries, tomatoes and flax seeds. It also boosts the immune system and alkalizes the body.

Chocolate Lover's Cacao Almond Smoothie

1 cup almond milk

1 teaspoon almond extract

⅓ cup almond butter

¾ to 1 teaspoon raw cacao

1 tablespoon raw honey

1 teaspoon super greens powder

1 tablespoon raw protein powder

Preparation

Place all ingredients in a blender and blend until smooth.

Adjust ingredients to taste and add ice for a thicker smoothie.

Tip: Add Chia Seeds to make a delicious pudding. Set in fridge for one hour.

What's the difference between cocoa and cacao? Raw cacao is made by cold pressing raw cocoa beans. Cocoa powder is raw cacao that's been roasted.

Breathe in Love

Breathe out Light

~ Debbie Danbrook, Healing Musician
Shakuhachi Flute Master

SUNRISE

Breakfast Fare

Happiness

is the prime directive.

~ *John Paul Copeland Artist/Musician/Father*

Nutty Homemade Granola

1 ½ cups rolled oats

1 ½ cups steel cut oats

¼ teaspoon Himalayan salt

¼ teaspoon cinnamon

¼ teaspoon nutmeg

2 tablespoons coconut oil

2 tablespoons raw honey

2 tablespoons maple syrup

½ teaspoon vanilla extract

½ cup of any mixture of the following: toasted pumpkin seeds, sunflower seeds, chopped walnuts, slivered almonds, goji berries

1 cup coconut or almond milk

Fresh berries

Fresh mint

Preparation

Preheat oven to 300°F.

In a bowl, mix oats, salt, cinnamon and nutmeg.

In a saucepan, warm the oil, honey and maple syrup. Whisk in vanilla extract. Pour the liquid over the oat mixture. Stir gently with a wooden spoon and finish mixing by hand.

Spread mixture on a 10" x 15" baking sheet. Bake 40 minutes, stirring every 10 minutes. Transfer pan to a rack; cool completely.

While the granola is baking, in a dry skillet, toast nuts and seeds until golden brown.

Place coconut milk, if using, in a blender with 1 cup water and blend until smooth

To serve, place granola in individual bowls, top with fresh berries, toasted seeds and/or nuts. Add almond or coconut milk and garnish with mint, if desired.

Serves 4

Winter Version: In a small saucepan, add cinnamon to almond milk to taste. Simmer on low for 2-3 minutes. Pour over Granola and serve.

Goji Berry and Chia Pudding

¼ cup chia seeds

¼ cup goji berries

1 teaspoon vanilla extract

1 tablespoon maple syrup

1½ cups unsweetened almond or coconut milk

Garnish with favourite fresh fruit

Preparation

Pour chia seeds and goji berries into a large bowl and mix in maple syrup and vanilla. Add almond milk and stir. Let mixture soak for 30 minutes.

Every 10 minutes, stir mixture to keep an even consistency. If the mixture is getting too thick, add more almond milk.

Serves 2-3

Goji berries have been used in Asia for generations to treat high blood pressure, fever, diabetes and age-related vision problems.

Maple French Toast

8 slices raisin bread

1 banana

½ cup almond or coconut milk

½ tablespoon maple syrup

½ tablespoon cinnamon

Preparation

Place bananas, almond or coconut milk, maple syrup and cinnamon in a blender. Blend on high until smooth. Heat non-stick skillet to medium. Pour batter into a bowl and dip bread slices in batter, soaking both sides. Cook bread slices one minute per side until golden brown. Serve with fresh fruit, chopped pecans, maple syrup and crispy tofu strips.

Serves 4

Crispy Tofu Strips

½ package firm tofu

1 tablespoon tamari

1 tablespoon toasted sesame oil

Dash liquid smoke

Preparation

Slice tofu into thin strips. Mix tamari, sesame oil and liquid smoke together. Marinade tofu strips at least 1 hour.
Heat grill or skillet to medium. Cook tofu on each side until crispy.

Serves 4

Banana Buckwheat Pancakes

1 cup brown rice flour

1 cup buckwheat flour

2 teaspoons baking powder

2 teaspoons baking soda

1 tablespoon cinnamon

Dash Himalayan salt

2 cups water

1 banana

1 tablespoon maple syrup

2 tablespoons grape seed oil

2 teaspoons fresh ginger, grated

Maple syrup for serving

½ cup blueberries and ¼ cup organic yogurt for serving

Buckwheat has a variety of healthful properties. It's an excellent plant source of easily digestive protein and contains all eight essential amino acids, so it's close to being a "complete" protein. Buckwheat is also high in fiber and B vitamins.

Preparation

Place brown rice flour, buckwheat flour, baking powder, baking soda, cinnamon, Himalayan salt, water, banana, maple syrup and ginger in a blender. Blend on high speed until smooth. Pour batter into a bowl. Heat oil in skillet; use a small ice cream scoop to pour batter onto skillet. Cook 1 minute per side, or until golden brown.

Serve with maple syrup, fresh blueberries and yogurt.

Serves 4

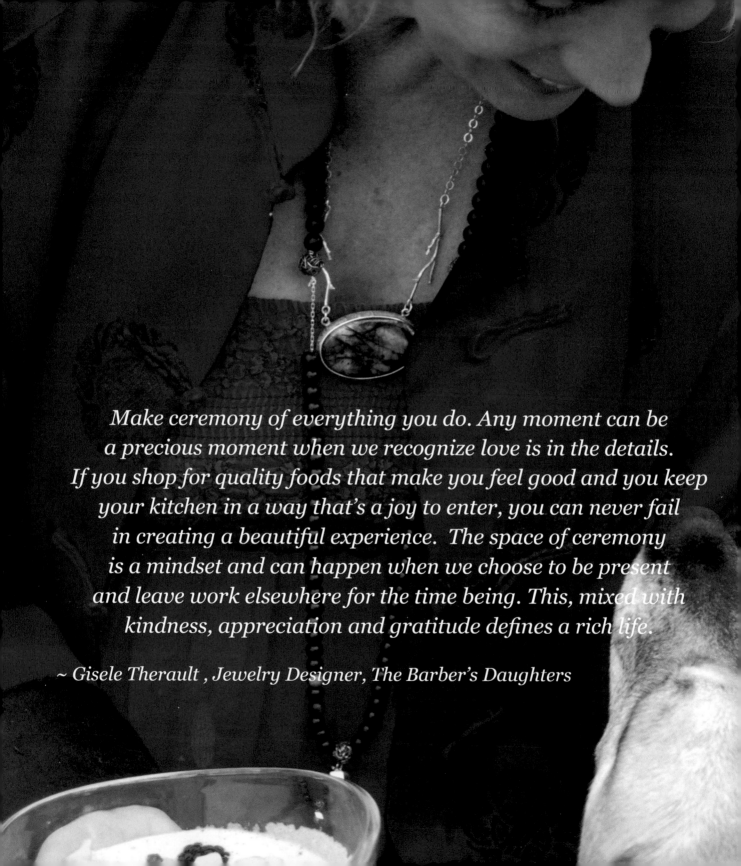

*Make ceremony of everything you do. Any moment can be
a precious moment when we recognize love is in the details.
If you shop for quality foods that make you feel good and you keep
your kitchen in a way that's a joy to enter, you can never fail
in creating a beautiful experience. The space of ceremony
is a mindset and can happen when we choose to be present
and leave work elsewhere for the time being. This, mixed with
kindness, appreciation and gratitude defines a rich life.*

~ Gisele Therault , Jewelry Designer, The Barber's Daughters

Gisele's Breakfast Schlop

1 tablespoon flax seed oil

Juice from ½ lemon

1 tablespoon maple syrup

⅓ to ½ cup of kefir or yogurt

2 tablespoons buckwheat groats

1 tablespoon black sesame seeds, roasted

¼ cup mango, chopped

¼ cup pomegranate juice

Walnuts

Preparation

Mix all the wet ingredients together.

Grind buckwheat grouts and black sesame seeds in a coffee grinder.

Then add to the wet mixture. Add fruit, and sprinkle with nuts.

My favourite way to start the day when not juicing is with a dish I call Breakfast Schlop. It's like eating cake batter for breakfast but it is super healthy.

Put down the smart phone and take a notification vacation.
Respond to the bells, whistles and chirps of your surroundings.
Download peace. Like adventure. Un-friend anxiety. Follow love.
Your life includes an unlimited data plan – don't worry about the bill.
Learning each day will keep your soul's battery forever charged.

~ Barb Shaw, recovering social (media) butterfly

ENERGY INSPIRATION

Mid-Day Meals
& Lighter Fare

Buckwheat Veggie Patties

½ onion
½ carrot
¼ small butternut squash
1 large broccoli floret
1 zucchini
4 baby potatoes
1 garlic clove
1 tablespoon buckwheat flour
1 tablespoon ground flax seeds
1 egg
1 teaspoon Himalayan salt
Pinch pepper

Preparation

Shred onion, carrot, squash, zucchini, broccoli and garlic in a food
processor with a medium size shedding blade, or finely julienne.
Mix together buckwheat and flax flours, salt, pepper and eggs. Mix into
shredded vegetables and let sit for 1 hour.
Heat grill or skillet to medium and oil lightly. Form vegetable mixture
into patties and grill on both sides until golden.

Serves 4

Farmer's Market Quiche with Potato Crust

Crust

2 medium red potatoes

1 teaspoon grape seed oil

1 teaspoon fresh lemon juice

½ teaspoon Himalayan salt

Pinch of black pepper

Quiche

½ cup onion, diced

½ cup broccoli, chopped

½ cup zucchini, chopped

½ cup kale, chopped

1 teaspoon grape seed oil

¼ cup diced tomatoes

4 eggs

¼ cup almond milk or coconut milk

½ teaspoon Himalayan salt

Pinch pepper

Topping

¼ cup vegan cheese or organic goat cheese

1 cup spinach, chopped

Preparation

Preheat oven to 400°F.

For the crust, wash and shred the potatoes in a food processor or grater. Mix in oil, lemon, salt and pepper. Evenly spread potato mixture on a lightly oiled deep dish casserole and bake for 15 minutes or until sides get crusty. Remove from oven and set aside. Reduce heat in oven to 350°F.

Heat the oil in a medium skillet and sauté the vegetables until they begin to soften. Spread over baked potato crust. Place eggs, almond milk, salt and pepper in blender and blend on high speed until mixture is fluffy. Pour over vegetables. Chop spinach and sprinkle on top, along with vegan cheese. Bake for 15 minutes, shake pan to re-distribute eggs and bake another 10-15 minutes until set.

Serves 4

Grail A-L-T Sandwich with Protein Dressing

1 avocado

¼ cup ground flaxseeds

½ teaspoon paprika

¼ teaspoon Himalayan salt

8 slices brown rice bread

Large tomato, sliced sprinkled with Himalayan salt

4 romaine lettuce leaves

4 dill pickles for serving

Preparation

Peel and slice avocados into wedges. Mix ground flax seeds, paprika and Himalayan salt. Coat avocado wedges with flax seed mixture. Bake in preheated oven for 30 minutes at 350° F.

Protein Dressing

2 tablespoons raw cashews

2 tablespoons raw sunflower seeds

1 teaspoon lemon juice

1 teaspoon maple syrup

Place cashews and sunflower seeds in a blender; add lemon juice and maple syrup and blend until smooth.

Sandwich Preparation

Toast two slices of brown rice bread and spread dressing on both slices. Add a slice of tomato and romaine lettuce. Place two avocado wedges in center and top with second toasted bread. Place a dill pickle on two skewers and secure sandwich on each side to hold together. Slice sandwich in half on an angle between the skewers to create two wedges.

Serves 4

Martin's Grilled Portobello Sandwich

2 slices brown rice bread
1 medium Portobello mushroom
1 tablespoon goat cheese spread (see preparation below)
¼ teaspoon white truffle-infused oil
2-3 slices ripe avocado

Preparation

Goat cheese spread: Mix 1 tablespoon goat cheese with ½ teaspoon
tamari and ½ teaspoon apple cider vinegar.
Brush truffle-infused oil on Portobello cap and grill until mushroom is
tender and juicy.
Grill or toast 2 slices brown rice bread. Spread goat cheese mixture
on both slices, top 1 slice with grilled Portobello and avocado. Slice
sandwich in half diagonally and serve.
Great with Martin's Sweet and Spicy Jicama Salad on page 84.

Serves 1

Toasted Buckwheat Tacos

Tacos

1 cup buckwheat

1 teaspoon grape seed oil

1 teaspoon Himalayan salt

½ teaspoon cumin

½ cup vegetable stock

1 tablespoon tamari

½ cup raw almonds

2 teaspoons vegetable stock

2 teaspoons olive oil

½ teaspoon cumin

½ teaspoon chili

½ teaspoon Himalayan salt

4 corn tortillas

8 romaine lettuce leaves

Salsa

½ cup corn

½ cup black beans, cooked

1 ½ cups organic tomatoes, diced

2 tablespoons cilantro

¼ medium onion, finely chopped

2 tablespoons chili powder

1 teaspoon Himalayan salt

1 teaspoon maple syrup

2 tablespoons red wine vinegar

Cashew Cream

¼ cup raw cashews

¼ cup raw almonds, sliced

Water to cover

¼ cup lemon juice

¼ cup goat milk yogurt (optional)

Preparation

Tacos

Panfry buckwheat in grape seed oil, Himalayan salt and ½ teaspoon cumin for 3-5 minutes. Add vegetable stock and tamari and simmer until cooked, but still crunchy. Mix raw almonds, vegetable stock, olive oil, ½ teaspoon cumin, chili powder and Himalayan salt in food processor until combined. Mix almond mixture with cooked buckwheat.

Salsa

In a bowl, mix together the corn, black beans, diced tomatoes, cilantro, onion, chili powder, Himalayan salt, maple syrup and red wine vinegar until well combined.

Cashew Cream

Place cashews, sliced almonds, lemon juice and goat milk (if using) in a blender. Cover with water and blend until smooth.

Lightly toast tortillas and line with lettuce leaves. Top with taco mixture and serve with salsa, cashew cream and Tomoko's Oh-So-Green Pea and Avocado Guacamole on page 142.

Serves 4

Quinoa Stuffed Tomatoes with Mixed Nut Crumble

¾ cup quinoa

1½ cups water

1 small onion, finely chopped

1 celery stalk, finely chopped

¼ cup green beans

½ zucchini, finely chopped

3-4 kale leaves, stalks removed and chopped

1 teaspoon grape seed oil

1 teaspoon Himalayan salt

1 teaspoon tamari

4 large tomatoes

Topping

¼ cup flaxseed flour

¼ cup sunflower seed flour

¼ cup brown rice breadcrumbs

½ teaspoon thyme

1 teaspoon coconut oil

Preparation

Rinse quinoa well under running water, place in saucepan, add water and cook until soft. Preheat oven to 350°F.

Cut off tops of each tomato and scoop out flesh; Set tomatoes aside.

Dice enough of the tomato flesh to equal ¾ cup.

Sauté onion, celery, green beans, zucchini, kale and Himalayan salt in grape seed oil just until vegetables start to soften. Mix in tamari, cooked quinoa and diced tomatoes. Keep warm.

For topping: Mix flax flour, sunflower seed flour, breadcrumbs, thyme and coconut oil until crumbly.

Stuff tomatoes with vegetable and quinoa mixture and sprinkle with topping. Transfer to a baking dish.

Bake for 10 minutes until tomatoes are soft.

Serves 4

Chickpea and Sweet Corn Croquettes

1 ½ cups chickpeas

2 cups water

1 zucchini, chopped

1 onion, chopped

½ cup brown rice bread crumbs

1 cup sweet corn

½ tablespoon cumin

1 teaspoon Himalayan salt

1 tablespoon extra virgin olive oil

Preparation

In a medium saucepan, cover chickpeas with water and let soak overnight. The next day, rinse chickpeas, cover with 2 cups of fresh water and cook on medium heat until tender, approximately 45 minutes. Preheat oven to 375°F.

Place zucchini, onions, breadcrumbs and cooked chickpeas in a food processor, add cumin, salt and olive oil. Blend only until mixed. Place in a medium bowl and mix in sweet corn. Oil a large baking sheet. Scoop out individual croquettes with an ice cream scoop, place onto baking sheet and flatten slightly. Bake 10 minutes, turn croquettes over and bake another 10 minutes until golden.

Serves 4

Black Bean Quesadilla with Cashew Cream

6 brown rice tortillas

½ celery stalk, finely chopped

½ carrot, finely diced

1 onion, finely chopped

1 red pepper, finely chopped

2 garlic cloves

½ tablespoon grape seed oil

1 tablespoon chili powder

½ tablespoon dairy free cheese

1 cup black beans, cooked

1½ cups diced tomatoes

Cashew Cream

¼ cup cashews
¼ cup slivered almonds
2 tablespoons lemon juice
Water to cover
Place cashews and almonds in a blender; cover with water and add lemon juice. Blend until smooth; set aside.

Preparation

Sauté chopped vegetables in grape seed oil and chili powder until vegetables are soft.
Mix cooked black beans and tomatoes into vegetable mixture.
Place one tortilla in a dry skillet, top with black bean and vegetable mixture and sprinkle with dairy free cheese. Cover with a second tortilla and weigh down to prevent the tortilla from curling up. Cook 5 minutes per side or until lightly brown and crispy. Remove from pan and cool slightly. Cut into wedges and serve with cashew cream and your favourite salsa.

Serves 4

"Seek and You Shall Find" ...

I believe these words are the greatest pearls of wisdom
and the secret to living a fulfilled life.
Spirit is like bread (manna).
Soul is like water (prana or life-force).
It is up to us to quench our hunger and thirst
for an enlightened, enriched life.
If we ask with a steady mind and a sincere heart, we
can receive that which we seek.
That is the promise of the Grail.

~ Madeleine Marentette, Founder
Grail Springs Retreat Centre for Wellbeing

FILL YOUR CUP
Soups for Sustenance

Madeleine's Roasted Tomato & Basil Soup

2 pounds tomatoes, quartered

3 tablespoons olive oil

4 cloves garlic peeled

1 quart vegetable stock

¼ cup chopped fresh basil

1 teaspoon balsamic vinegar

Himalayan salt coarsley ground to taste

Fresh ground pepper

1 tablespoon of lemon juice to taste

Organic yogurt to garnish

Preparation

Preheat oven to 375°F.

Place the quartered tomatoes and whole garlic cloves in a bowl.
Drizzle with oil and toss with salt. Gently mix together until garlic
becomes aromatic. Pour onto a foil-lined baking sheet. Roast for 20-30
minutes until the tomato and garlic look slightly browned. Remove
from oven. Carefully stir in the chopped basil. Bake for another 10-15
minutes. Cool for 5 minutes, then remove the tomato skins.

Pour all ingredients from the baking tray into a food processor, add
stock and vinegar; gently pulse until desired consistency, leaving
it somewhat rustic and textured. Season to taste with lemon juice
and pepper. Serve either hot or cold. Garnish with organic yogurt if
desired.

Serves 4

Mushroom Soup with Garlic Croutons

1 medium onion, chopped
2 large celery stalks, chopped
3 Portobello mushroom caps, chopped
1 garlic clove, crushed
½ tablespoon coconut oil
½ tablespoon Himalayan salt
Pinch pepper
4 cups vegetable stock
1 cup coconut milk

2 tablespoons brown rice flour
2 tablespoons Italian parsley,
   chopped for serving
Garlic Croutons
3 slices brown rice bread, cubed
1 tablespoon garlic oil OR
1 tablespoon grapeseed oil
   with 1 clove crushed garlic

Preparation

Sauté onion, celery, mushrooms, garlic, Himalayan salt and pepper in coconut oil until vegetables are soft. Add vegetable stock and simmer 20-30 minutes.

Mix brown rice flour and coconut milk until smooth. Add to soup and stir until soup starts to thicken.

Serve with chopped parsley and garlic croutons.

To prepare the croutons, place brown rice bread cubes in a skillet with garlic oil and toast on all sides until bread is light brown and crunchy.

Serves 4

Mother Harmony's Moroccan Peanut Tomato Soup

2 ½ cups crunchy peanut butter

2 onions, finely chopped

2 (19 ounce) cans chopped tomatoes

2 tablespoon extra virgin olive oil

½ cup tomato paste

¼ cup balsamic vinegar

1 - 2 tablespoon maple syrup

2 tablespoons chili powder

1 tablespoon cumin

1 teaspoon black pepper

1 teaspoon Thai red chili paste

3 cups water

Preparation

In a large saucepan or stockpot, sauté onion and garlic in olive oil.

Add all remaining ingredients except water.

Bring to a slow simmer, stirring frequently to prevent sticking.

Stir in water. Simmer 15 minutes, stirring occasionally.

Serves 8

Tara's Rainbow Soup

2 - 3 tablespoons olive or other cooking oil

3 cloves garlic, finely chopped

4 large carrots, thinly sliced

2 large stalks celery, finely chopped

1 large red onion, finely chopped

1 (5½ ounce) can tomato paste, diluted in 2 cups water

1 (19 ounce) can chopped regular or plum tomatoes
 (or fresh tomatoes)

Up to 10 cups water

1 (19 ounce) can red kidney beans drained

2 tablespoons dried parsley

½ teaspoon dried rosemary

1 teaspoon sweet or hot paprika

1 teaspoon dried basil

½ teaspoon dried thyme, or to taste

1 cup frozen or fresh corn kernels

1 cup peas, fresh or frozen

1 cup kale leaves, chopped

1 small red pepper, diced

1 small yellow pepper, diced

1 small orange pepper, diced

½ cup rainbow chard, finely chopped

2 medium potatoes, cubed

½ cup rice or pasta

Grated Romano cheese or non-dairy cheese for serving

Preparation

Heat the oil in a large deep pot; braise the garlic, carrots, onions and celery in the oil on medium high heat for about 10 minutes.

Add 6 cups of water, then the diluted tomato paste, spices and other vegetables. Bring to a boil then simmer for about one and half hours. Add each vegetable in smaller amounts at first and judge if it needs more or less. Taste as you go. Add more water as it cooks if it starts to thicken too much.

Serves 8-10

A sprinkling of love expressed daily to the world and to yourself will sustain a succulent life forever remembered.

~ Shawna Ross, Spiritual Counselor

Corn Harvest Chowder

4 fresh cobs of corn, kernels removed from cob
(or 2 cups frozen corn, rinsed)
1 large onion, diced
1 large carrot, diced
2 celery stalks, diced
8 new baby potatoes, cubed
4 cups vegetable stock
1 cup coconut milk
2 tablespoons brown rice flour
2 tablespoons Himalayan salt
Pinch pepper
1 tablespoon coconut oil
¼ cup fresh parsley, finely chopped
Chili flakes for serving (optional)

Preparation

Sauté onion, carrots and celery in coconut oil and 1 tablespoon
Himalayan salt, until vegetables start to soften. Add potatoes and
simmer until potatoes are soft.
Place vegetable stock, coconut milk, corn, brown rice flour, 1
tablespoon Himalayan salt and pepper in a blender and process until
creamy. Add to soup and cook until soup starts to thicken.
Stir in parsley just before serving. Sprinkle with chili flakes, if using.

Serves 8

Butternut Squash and Red Lentil Soup

4 cups butternut squash, peeled and chopped

1 medium onion, chopped

1 carrot, finely chopped

1 celery stalk, sliced

3 garlic cloves, finely chopped

1½ teaspoons mild curry powder

1 teaspoon Himalayan salt

1 tablespoon coconut oil

1 cup red lentils, rinsed

4 cups vegetable stock

1 cup coconut milk

Preparation

Heat oil in a large stockpot, lightly sauté vegetables, curry powder and 1 teaspoon of Himalayan salt in coconut oil, until vegetables start to soften. Add lentils, vegetable stock and remaining salt and simmer until vegetables are tender, 20-30 minutes.

Puree in blender or with immersion blender until smooth. Add coconut milk and simmer 5 minutes.

Serves 8

The health benefits of lentils include a high protein content, rich in amino acids, vitamins and minerals. Lentils can improve digestion, assist with weight loss and help to maintain a healthy nervous system.

Beet and Ginger Borscht

1 medium onion, chopped

1 carrot, chopped

1 celery stalk, sliced

1 parsnip, peeled and chopped

½ daikon, peeled and chopped

3 large beets (save peels)

½" piece of ginger

¼ head red cabbage

1 tablespoon extra virgin olive oil

1 teaspoon Himalayan salt

8 cups vegetable stock

1½ cups diced tomatoes

1 tablespoon Himalayan salt

Preparation

Sauté vegetables in olive oil and 1 teaspoon of salt, until vegetables begin to soften.

In a separate pot, heat vegetable stock with beet peels and simmer for a few minutes. Strain peels, reserving stock.

Add stock to sautéed vegetables, stir in tomatoes and 1 tablespoon salt and simmer until vegetables are tender.

Serves 8

Chunky Leek and Sweet Potato Miso Soup

1 large sweet potato, peeled and finely chopped
2 leeks (white part only), washed and finely sliced
2 garlic cloves, sliced
4 cups vegetable broth
1 tablespoon organic brown rice miso, melted in ½ cup of hot water
1 teaspoon Himalayan salt
1 teaspoon nutritional yeast

Sweet Potatoes, high in vitamins B6, C, D, iron and magnesium, are linked to heart health, and increased energy.

Preparation

Place sweet potatoes, leeks, vegetable broth, salt and nutritional yeast in large stockpot; add the softened miso. Bring to a boil, reduce temperature and simmer soup until potatoes are soft, 15-20 minutes. Serve as is or blend in food processor for a creamy version.

Serves 4

Trust in Divine Order. Know there are no accidents.
Everything, without exception, has a divine reason to Be.
Look closely for the gifts, the lessons of each life experience and
what you can learn from it. Sometimes it requires surrender.
You will be left with certainty that the outcome is perfect,
because you have trusted that Divine Order
is always conspiring for goodness.

~ Vera Lopez, Shamanic Minister and Sacred Travel Guide, Machu Pichu

Triple Green Goddess Soup

1 large head broccoli, chopped
2 medium onions, chopped
3 stalks celery, chopped
8 cups vegetable broth
1 tablespoon grape seed oil

1 tablespoon Himalayan salt
Pinch pepper
½ cup green sweet peas
2 cups spinach, washed
Dill or chili flakes for serving

Preparation

In a large stockpot, sauté onion in grape seed oil until translucent.
Add celery and broccoli, and sauté until celery starts to soften. Add
vegetable broth, season with salt and pepper. Bring to a boil. Reduce
heat and simmer until vegetables are soft. Add peas and spinach in the
last 5 minutes of cooking.
Transfer soup to a blender and blend until smooth. Adjust seasonings.
Ladle into soup bowls, sprinkle with dill or spice it up with chili flakes.

Serves 8

In every Nation, in every Clan
The Elders to a person
Whether women or a man
Shared a common truth
One truth to understand
That the spirit of the people is equal
To the Power of The Land.

Excerpt from 'The Power of the Land'

~ *Duke Redbird, Saugeen First Nation, Poet, Activist*

Three Sisters Soup

2 cups fresh corn, removed from cob

2 cups fresh green beans, trimmed and cut into 1½ inch pieces

2 cups butternut squash, chopped

1 medium sweet onion, chopped

6 garlic cloves

6 cups vegetable broth

3 sprigs of fresh rosemary or ½ teaspoon dry

2-3 sprigs of fresh thyme or ½ teaspoon dry

2-3 sprigs fresh basil or ½ teaspoon dry

1 cup red potato, washed and cubed

2 – 3 bay leaves

1 tablespoon salt

½ fresh lemon, juiced

¼ cup grape seed oil

Preparation

Sauté the onion in oil until translucent; add the garlic and sauté 1 minute. Add the squash next and sauté 2 minutes. Add green beans and sauté for 2 minutes, and then add corn, salt and herbs and sauté another minute. Keep stirring and do not let the soup burn.
Add vegetable broth, potato, herbs, salt and simmer covered for 1½ hours. Remove herb sprigs before serving.

Serves 6-8

The Three Sisters Story

The Native American 'three sisters' are the spirits of corn (maize), beans, and squash. The 'three sisters' term dates back to the 19th century may have first originated by the Iroquois tribe in the Northeast. Three Sisters...the corn stalk, the bean vine and the squash would all be planted together in one mound. The corn stalk gives support for the beans to climb on. The beans take nitrogen from the air and deliver it to the ground for the corn and squash to grow big and healthy. The squash plant with its large broad leaves prevents weeds and preserves moisture for all three of them.

By all three working together they can be more and do more then they could by themselves.

We can always do more by helping each other.

Orange, Carrot and Ginger Soup

1 medium onion, chopped

8 carrots, chopped

1 celery stalk, chopped

1 teaspoon grape seed oil

8 cups vegetable stock

¼ cup ginger, chopped

1 tablespoon Himalayan salt

1 teaspoon orange peel, grated

1 cup orange juice

Pinch pepper

½ cup shredded fresh beets for garnish

Preparation

Sauté onion, carrots and celery in grape seed oil until vegetables start to soften. Add vegetable stock, ginger and salt. Simmer until vegetables are soft, 20-30 minutes.

Blend in food processor or blender until smooth. Mix in orange peel, orange juice and dash of pepper.

Sprinkle with grated beets and serve.

Serves 8

Carrots are a source of potassium that can relax blood vessels and arteries to increase blood flow and circulation. Yes, and the vitamin A in carrots means they're good for your eyesight too!

Butternut Squash and Apple Soup

1 tablespoon olive oil
2 medium red onions, chopped
1 large butternut squash, peeled,
 seeds removed, cut in cubes
3 apples, cored (do not peel)

5-8 cinnamon sticks
Himalayan salt and pepper to taste
2 – 3 cups vegetable broth
1 tablespoon toasted pumpkin seeds

Preparation

Sauté onions in olive oil until translucent; add squash and sauté
a bit more. Add apples, cinnamon sticks and pepper. Cover with
water and bring to a boil. Lower heat and let simmer for 1 hour.
Remove from heat and let cool for 30 minutes.
Remove cinnamon sticks and purée in blender or food processor.
Serve with sprinkled toasted pumpkin seeds.

Serves 6-8

*Stir with love.
It's the secret
ingredient that
transforms food
into beautiful,
healthy energy.*

~ Chef Tomoko

Tomoko's Healing Vegetable Soup with Ginger and Lemon Zest

¼ cup onion, finely chopped

¼ cup carrot, finely chopped

¼ cup celery, finely chopped

¼ cup daikon, finely chopped

¼ cup red pepper, finely chopped

¼ cup zucchini, finely chopped

¼ cup napa cabbage, shredded

¼ cup freshly grated ginger, plus extra for serving

1 tablespoon grape seed oil

8 cups vegetable broth

1 tablespoon Himalayan salt

¼ cup lemon juice

½ tablespoon lemon rind, grated

Lemon slices for serving

3 finely sliced green onions and chili flakes for serving

Preparation

In a large stockpot, sauté vegetables for 5-10 minutes in grape seed oil. Add vegetable broth, salt, lemon juice and lemon rind. Bring to a boil. Reduce heat and simmer 20-30 minutes, or until vegetables are tender. To serve, ladle into bowls, float a lemon slice on top and sprinkle with extra fresh ginger, green onions and chili flakes.

Serves 8

This cup-a-soup is a great post-workout recovery beverage that you can make ahead of time and freeze in batches.
It is designed to restore fluids lost in sweat, while the tomato juice base helps to repair damaged muscle tissue.

Hearty Rejuvenating Tomato Cup-a-Soup with Lemon and Spice

½ red pepper, chopped
½ yellow pepper, chopped
1 carrot, diced
1 celery stalk, sliced
¼ fennel bulb, chopped
2 garlic cloves, finely chopped
½ cup fresh basil, finely chopped
½ cup fresh parsley, finely chopped
1 bay leaf

1 teaspoon fresh rosemary, chopped
½ teaspoon chili powder
4 cups tomato based vegetable juice (no sodium)
2 cups fresh tomatoes, diced
2 cups vegetable stock
½ tablespoon Himalayan salt
½ cup lemon juice
Tabasco and fresh basil for serving

Preparation

Place vegetables, basil, parsley, bay leaf, rosemary, chili powder, juice, tomatoes, vegetable stock and salt in large stockpot. Bring to a boil, reduce heat and simmer until vegetables are soft, about 1 -1½ hours.
Blend in blender or with immersion blender until smooth.
Add lemon juice and adjust seasonings.
Serve sprinkled with chopped fresh basil and dash of Tabasco sauce.

Serves 8

Lemons have antiviral, antibacterial and immune boosting properties. Lemon juice is a liver cleanser, digestive aid and it fights infection. Ancient Egyptians ate lemons as protection against many poisons.

Follow your heart into your passion and then let it guide you from experience to experience. Trust everything that comes your way, even those things that seem to be unrelated to your desires.
The setbacks, the 'wrong' turns and distractions all add up the unique ingredients you bring to your greatest offering... You. What you do and create in the world is important but who you become in the process is the most valuable part of this life journey. There are no mistakes. Simply allow the experiences that life brings push you to grow into an ever better, stronger, more mature, loving, joyous and gracious version of yourself. Every experience can move us toward our goal in mysterious ways if we allow it, going with life's flow. If a treasured dream doesn't work, never give up. Trust you are still being led toward that dream. Each experience that comes your way is a necessary ingredient to our greatest recipe... Yourself."
~ Michael Moon, Healing Musician

VITALITY SALADS

Greens & More

During the Inca Empire quinoa was called "the Mother of all Grains" and still grows abundantly in the sacred mountains of Peru. Considered a complete protein, this grain has reached superfood status all over the world. Prepared just like rice, quinoa can be tossed into salads or stand alone as a meal with any variety of chopped vegetables and a favourite dressing.

Quinoa and Roasted Walnut Salad with Red Wine Vinaigrette

1 cup quinoa

2 cups water

½ red pepper, finely chopped

½ green pepper, finely chopped

1 carrot, grated

½ cucumber, finely chopped

½ cup romaine lettuce, finely chopped

2 garlic cloves, minced

½ cup walnuts halves

Red Wine Vinaigrette

½ cup red wine vinegar

1 tablespoon walnut oil

1 tablespoon maple syrup

¼ cup red onion, chopped

2 garlic cloves

1 teaspoon Himalayan salt

Pinch pepper

Preparation

Rinse quinoa well under cool running water. Transfer to a stockpot; add water and cook on medium heat until water is absorbed and quinoa is cooked, 12-15 minutes. Fluff with a fork and allow quinoa to cool.

Roast walnuts in a dry skilled until light brown, 2-3 minutes.

To make vinaigrette, place all ingredients in a blender. Blend until smooth.

Mix quinoa and vegetables with red wine vinaigrette and let marinade for at least 1 hour before serving.

Sprinkle with roasted walnuts and serve.

Also great over arugula!

Serves 4

Martin's Sweet and Spicy Jicama Salad

1 jicama
1 carrot
12 cherry tomatoes
1 head romaine lettuce

Dressing

½ cup fresh lime juice
2 tablespoons vanilla extract
1 tablespoon chili paste
Himalayan salt and pepper to taste

Jicama is full of health-boosting vitamins and minerals including potassium - an all important trace mineral for sustaining health. Jicama helps to boost the immune system, reduce inflammation and support skin and eye health.

Preparation

Wash and dry the lettuce; peel and julienne the jicama and carrot.
Place dressing ingredients in a glass jar and shake to combine.
Divide lettuce between serving plates, top with jicama, carrot and cherry tomatoes. Pour dressing over salad and serve.

Serves 6

Carrot, Orange and Mango Salad

2 carrots, shredded or julienned
1 celery stalk, thinly sliced
1 tablespoon Italian parsley, finely chopped
1 tablespoon pumpkin seeds
1 orange, julienned
1 mango, julienned

Dressing

½ tablespoon apple cider vinegar
½ tablespoon extra virgin olive oil
½ tablespoon agave nectar
½ teaspoon Himalayan salt

Preparation

Roast pumpkin seeds in a dry skillet until light brown. Cool.
Mix together carrots, celery, parsley, orange, mango, apple cider vinegar,
olive oil, agave nectar, Himalayan salt and cooled roasted pumpkin seeds.
Allow to marinade for 1 hour before serving.

Serves 4

Apple cider vinegar is an excellent aid for losing excess weight. It boosts your metabolism to work at its best and burn extra calories.

Hail To The Kale Salad

½ bunch kale

Dressing

2 tablespoons fresh lemon juice

2 tablespoons agave nectar

2 tablespoons apple cider vinegar

3 tablespoons extra virgin olive oil

1 tablespoon Dijon mustard

½ teaspoon Himalayan salt

Dash pepper

1 tablespoon hemp seeds

Pumpkin seeds, pine nuts and grape tomatoes for serving

Preparation

Wash and remove stalks from kale, cut into ribbons.

In blender, blend dressing ingredients for 1 minute on high speed.

Stir in hemp seeds by hand.

Pour over kale and marinate for at least 1 hour before serving.

Toss in pumpkin seeds, pine nuts, grape tomatoes and serve.

Serves 4

Kale is one of the most nutrient dense foods on the planet. Loaded with antioxidants, high in mineral content, kale also contains vitamin C and lots of vitamin K, which helps to prevent heart disease and osteoporosis.

Yvette's Quinoa Cleanser Salad

1 cup quinoa

2 cups water

1 ½ cups kale leaves, finely chopped

Marinade

1-2 garlic cloves, minced

¼ cup extra virgin olive oil

¼ cup lemon juice

½ teaspoon Himalayan salt

Dash of cayenne pepper (optional)

Baby salad greens

1 ½ cups Italian flat leaf parsley, finely chopped

4 green onions, chopped

¼ cup fresh basil, chopped

Fresh tomatoes.

Preparation

Rinse quinoa well in a fine sieve under cold running water. Transfer to pot, add water and bring to a boil. Reduce heat, cover and simmer until quinoa is tender, approximately 15 minutes. Remove from heat and let sit covered for 5-10 minutes, then fluff with a fork. Allow quinoa to cool.

Place chopped kale and quinoa in a mixing bowl, toss with marinade and let sit for 1 hour.

When ready to serve toss with remaining ingredients and serve.

Serves 4-6

Sweet Curry Cauliflower Salad

½ cup celery, chopped
½ cup red pepper, chopped
1 small onion, diced
½ head cauliflower, chopped
1 tablespoon Italian parsley, minced

Dressing

2 tablespoons apple cider vinegar
¼ cup extra virgin olive oil
1 tablespoon raw honey
2 garlic cloves
½ teaspoon curry powder
½ teaspoon Himalayan salt
Pinch pepper

Preparation

Place apple cider vinegar, olive oil, honey, garlic, curry powder,
Himalayan salt and pepper in a blender and pulse until creamy.
Add dressing to chopped vegetables and let marinate at least 1 hour.
Serve sprinkled with parsley.

Serves 4

Summer Harvest Salad

8 cups greens (spring mix, spinach, baby kale, arugula)
1 avocado, chopped
2 green onions, chopped
½ cucumber, cut into chunks
$1/3$ cup slivered almonds or pine nuts
1 cup fresh berries

Dressing

⅓ cup walnut oil
3 tablespoons apple cider vinegar
1 teaspoon prepared Dijon mustard
Himalayan salt, and pepper to taste
Top with fresh sprouts

Preparation

Roast almonds or pine nuts in a dry skillet until fragrant and light brown. Rinse greens and spin in salad spinner; pat dry with a paper towel. Mix in avocado, green onions, cucumber and roasted nuts. In a blender mix walnut oil, apple cider vinegar, Dijon mustard and blend for 1 minute. Adjust to taste. Toss into salad adding a dash of salt and pepper. Top individual servings with fresh berries and sprouts. Serve immediately.

Serves 4

Variations

Mix things up with any freshly harvested summer ingredients:
dill, basil, radish, apple, celery, etc.

Big Fat Greek Tofu Salad

8 cups romaine lettuce

1 English cucumber, chopped

1 red pepper, chopped

1 cup cherry tomatoes cut in half

12 Kalamata olives

½ cup fresh oregano leaves, chopped

Dressing

1 garlic clove

½ onion, chopped

¼ cup balsamic vinegar

½ tablespoon oregano, dried

¼ cup sundried tomatoes, soaked in water

1 teaspoon Dijon mustard

2 tablespoons fresh lemon juice

1 teaspoon agave nectar, raw honey or maple syrup

¼ teaspoon Himalayan salt

Dash pepper

¼ cup extra virgin olive oil

Tofu Crumble

½ package firm tofu

1 tablespoon fresh lemon juice

1 tablespoon nutritional yeast

2 garlic cloves

1 teaspoon Himalayan salt

Preparation

Wash and dry lettuce; place in a bowl with cucumbers, peppers, tomatoes and oregano.

To make dressing, place garlic and onion in food processor and mix; add balsamic vinegar, oregano, sundried tomatoes, Dijon mustard, lemon juice, agave nectar, Himalayan salt and pepper. With machine running, slowly add olive oil until dressing is smooth.

To make tofu crumble, place tofu, lemon juice, nutritional yeast, garlic and Himalayan salt in a bowl and mix by hand, until mixture has a consistency similar to feta cheese.

To serve, divide lettuce between serving plates, add cucumbers, peppers, tomatoes and olives. Sprinkle with tofu crumble and oregano leaves. Pour dressing over salad and serve immediately.

Serves 4

In the Mediterranean where olive oil is produced and used extensively, heart disease is very rare. Researchers have discovered that olive oil is rich in antioxidants, that it decreases inflammation and it improves functioning of blood vessel lining. Recent research has shown that olive oil can help prevent the build-up of plaque in brain cells which may cause Alzheimer's Disease

Herb and Garlic Potato Salad

1 pound red or yellow baby potatoes
¼ cup green onion, thinly sliced
¼ cup celery, thinly sliced
¼ cup fresh Italian parsley, finely chopped
1 tablespoon fresh thyme, finely chopped or 1 teaspoon dried
1 tablespoon fresh basil, finely chopped
Cherry tomatoes, halved
Hemp seeds for serving

Dressing

1 tablespoon Dijon mustard
2 tablespoons apple cider vinegar
1 tablespoon lemon juice
1 garlic clove, minced
3 tablespoons olive oil
Himalayan salt and pepper to taste

Preparation

Wash and quarter the potatoes. Place them in a pot, cover with water, add salt and bring to a boil. Reduce heat and simmer until potatoes are tender, but not overcooked. Drain and allow them to cool.
Place all dressing ingredients in a mixing bowl and mix gently. Adjust seasonings. Toss all ingredients in with the prepared dressing. Let salad marinade in refrigerator for at least one hour or overnight.
Serve with sprinkle of hemp seeds.

Serves 4

Spinach, Fennel and Strawberry Salad with Cranberry Vinaigrette

8 cups baby spinach leaves
½ cucumber, thinly sliced
¼ fennel bulb, thinly sliced
8 strawberries
¼ cup pumpkin seeds

Cranberry Vinaigrette

¼ cup dried cranberries
¼ small red onion, chopped
2 tablespoons apple cider vinegar
1 tablespoon agave nectar
¼ cup extra virgin olive oil
1 tablespoon fresh lemon juice
¼ teaspoon Himalayan salt
Pinch pepper

Preparation

Wash and dry spinach leaves; slice cucumbers and fennel.
Place dried cranberries, chopped red onion, apple cider vinegar, agave nectar, olive oil, lemon juice, Himalayan salt and pepper in blender and blend until smooth.
Divide spinach between serving plates, top with cucumbers, fennel, and strawberries. Pour vinaigrette over salad and sprinkle with pumpkin seeds and flowers. Serve immediately.

Serves 4

Cucumber Tomato Salad

1 cucumber, thinly sliced
½ medium red onion, thinly sliced
1 medium ripe tomato, chopped

Dressing
Juice of ½ lemon
1½ tablespoons apple cider vinegar
3 tablespoons grape seed oil
½ teaspoon Himalayan salt
1 teaspoon raw sugar

Preparation

Place cucumber, tomato and onions in a large bowl; mix together gently and let sit to allow the juices to blend.
Mix all the ingredients for the dressing in a blender. Pour over the tomato, cucumber and onion. Gently stir and let stand for at least 30 minutes before serving.

Serves 2

Red Cabbage Coleslaw

½ small head red cabbage
1 celery stalk, finely sliced
1 carrot julienned

Dressing

¼ cup apple cider vinegar
¼ cup extra virgin olive oil
¼ cup maple syrup
Himalayan salt and pepper to taste

Preparation

Finely slice or shred cabbage in food processor. Toss in sliced celery
and carrot. Mix apple cider vinegar, olive oil, maple syrup, Himalayan
salt and pepper in blender on high speed.
Pour dressing over cabbage and marinate 1 hour before serving.

Serves 4

David Maracle's Wild Rice, Cranberry and Lime Salad

2 cups wild black rice

1 cup cranberries

5 leaves fresh basil

1 small cucumber

1 red pepper

1/3 cup sesame seeds or pine nuts

7 dried apricots

1 large carrot

5 sprigs fresh parsley

1 medium sweet purple onion

Preparation

Rinse wild rice well and follow cooking instructions. Bring the pot of rice to a boil. When it starts to boil add 1/3 of the cranberries. Cover and simmer until rice is ready. You may need to add more water to the rice, so make sure to keep an eye on it. Once the rice starts to open and curl up, it's ready to be drained. Place the rice in a glass bowl and let chill in the refrigerator for 30 minutes.

Take all the remaining fresh ingredients and chop finely together. Once the rice has cooled, add all of the chopped mixture to the cold rice.

Dressing

½ cup extra virgin olive oil
¼ cup maple syrup
⅓ cup balsamic vinegar
4 tablespoons lime juice
Fresh ground pepper

Mix all of the above ingredients together. Pour over rice and toss.
Keep refrigerated until ready to serve.

Serves 4

Nia:kowa ne kukwa ~Thank you for the food

My advice to the younger you...
surround yourself with people that inspire you
and let go of trying to be understood by the many.

~ Janet Sinclair, Rose Wing Warrior

THE MAIN VERVE
Hearty Meals

Sundried Tomato and Eggplant Casserole

1 cup onion, chopped

1 cup carrots, diced

1 cup celery, chopped

1 cup green vegetables (peas, broccoli, green beans), chopped

1 cup sundried tomatoes

1 tablespoon olive oil

1 cup millet

2 cups water

1 cup vegetable stock

1 cup tomato juice

1 cup fresh oregano, finely chopped

1 tablespoon paprika

½ tablespoon Himalayan salt

2 medium eggplants, thinly sliced

1 tablespoon olive oil

White Sauce

1 cup almond milk

¼ cup nutritional yeast

1 tablespoon brown rice flour

½ tablespoon Himalayan salt

Pinch pepper

2 eggs

½ cup vegan cheese

1 garlic clove

Eggplants are a rich source of vitamin C, K, B6, thiamin, niacin, magnesium, fiber, folic acid and potassium.

Preparation

Soak sundried tomatoes in water for 30 minutes or longer. Drain and finely chop.

Cook millet in water until tender, 10-12 minutes.

Brush eggplant with olive oil and grill or broil on both sides until tender.

Preheat oven to 350°F.

Sauté the vegetables in olive oil until soft.

Mix in sundried tomatoes, vegetable stock, tomato juice, oregano, paprika and Himalayan salt.

Mix in cooked millet and transfer to a casserole dish.

Place grilled eggplant on top of vegetables.

White Sauce

Blend all ingredients in a blender on high speed for one minute.

Pour white sauce over casserole. Bake for 40 minutes, until casserole is set.

Cut into squares and serve.

Serves 8

Chef Samantha Gowing's Sea Vegetables with Kelp Noodles, Nuts, Sprouts and Seeds

1 packet kelp noodles, rinsed and drained
    *use cooked vermicelli if unavailable
¼ cup red cabbage, shredded
½ cup assorted sprouts – mung, chickpea, lentil
1 toasted nori sheet, shredded
1 tablespoon wakame seaweed, soaked and drained
1 cup activated almonds, roughly chopped
1 teaspoon black sesame seeds
1 tablespoon pickled ginger, shredded
1 umeboshi plum, pitted, roughly chopped

Dressing

1/3 cup walnut or macadamia nut oil	1 teaspoon miso paste
2 tablespoons mirin	1 teaspoon grated ginger
1 tablespoon tamari	1 lime, zest and juice

Rinse and refresh kelp noodles, drain and set aside.
Combine cabbage, sprouts, seaweed, almonds and sesame seeds.
Add kelp noodles and toss well.
Whisk dressing ingredients together well and blend into noodles.
Arrange in individual bowls, garnish with pickled ginger and umeboshi plum.

Serves 4

Brown Rice Sushi with Pickled Ginger

1 cup brown rice

2 cups water

⅓ cup brown rice vinegar

1 tablespoon raw sugar or honey

1 teaspoon Himalayan salt

4 romaine lettuce leaves, shredded

⅓ cup spinach, shredded

⅓ cup carrots, grated

1 cucumber, thinly sliced

¼ red pepper, thinly sliced

¼ yellow pepper, thinly sliced

1 avocado cut in wedges

4 nori sheets

Pickled ginger

⅓ cup sliced ginger

2 teaspoons brown rice vinegar or apple cider vinegar

1 teaspoon raw sugar

Sprinkle of Himalayan salt

Preparation

Rice

Soak brown rice in water 2 hours to overnight. Cook until rice is tender. Transfer rice to a wooden bowl.*

In a small saucepan on low heat, dissolve brown rice vinegar, raw sugar and Himalayan salt. Mix vinegar mixture into cooked rice while rice is still warm.

*Using a wooden bowl will make the rice mixture sticky.

Pickled Ginger

Peel and slice ginger, sprinkle with Himalayan salt, then mix in vinegar and sugar.

Top each nori sheet with rice mixture, romaine lettuce, spinach, grated carrots, red and yellow pepper, cucumber and avocados. Roll tightly and cut into 8-10 rounds each.

Serve with sliced pickled ginger.

Serves 4

Martin's Moroccan Curry

1 tablespoon dried ginger

1 tablespoon cumin

1 tablespoon chili powder

1 tablespoon 5-spice powder

1 tablespoon turmeric

1 tablespoon dried mint

1 tablespoon basil

1 tablespoon oregano

2 cans coconut milk

1 cup dried apricots

2 fresh basil leaves

2 bay leaves

1 cup broccoli, chopped

1 cup carrots, diced

1 cup kale, chopped

1 tablespoon grape seed oil

1 package firm tofu

2 tablespoons sesame oil

Preparation

Mix together ginger, cumin, chili powder, 5-spice powder, turmeric, mint, basil and oregano. Place in saucepan with coconut milk, dried apricots, fresh basil and bay leaf. Bring to a boil, reduce heat and simmer until apricots are soft. Remove bay leaf.

In a separate pan, sauté broccoli, carrots and kale in grape seed oil until vegetables are tender.

Cut tofu into bite sized squares, brush with sesame oil and grill on both sides until golden.

Mix together sautéed vegetables, grilled tofu and coconut milk mixture and simmer a few minutes to combine flavors.

Serves 4

Mung Bean Chili

1 medium onion, finely chopped

2 stalks celery, finely chopped

2 carrots, finely chopped

½ green pepper, finely chopped

½ red pepper, finely chopped

3 garlic cloves, finely chopped

1 tablespoon olive oil

1 tablespoon chili powder, or more to taste

2 tablespoons cumin

1 tablespoon Himalayan salt

Dash pepper

½ cup brown basmati rice, cooked

1 cup water

2 cups crushed tomatoes, drained

5 cups vegetable stock

4 cups soaked mung beans

Preparation

Place mung beans in a bowl or glass jar, cover with water and soak overnight.

Preheat oven to 350°F.

Cook millet in water, until soft, set aside.

Sauté onions, celery, carrots, peppers and garlic in olive oil until vegetables are soft, 20-30 minutes. Mix in cooked rice.

Transfer cooked vegetables into a deep baking dish, add drained crushed tomatoes and vegetable stock and mix well.

Cover and bake for 1½ to 2 hours or until vegetables are tender.

Serve with dairy free cheese.

Serves 8

The need to thrive is beyond healthy food, yoga moves and green smoothies. It is about finding our innate self, our essential nature, and allowing all of these aspects to integrate into ourselves. This is the ultimate pathway to whole happiness.

~ Chef Samantha Gowing, Australia's Leading Spa Chef

Chef Samantha Gowing's Adzuki, Pumpkin and Tamarind Curry

2 tablespoons coconut oil

1 teaspoon mustard seeds

½ teaspoon cumin seeds

1 Spanish onion, diced finely

8 oz adzuki beans, soaked overnight

10 oz tamarind water

2 green chillies, seed removed, chopped finely

7 oz pumpkin, skin & seed removed, cut into ¾ inch dice

¼ teaspoon ground coriander

¼ teaspoon ground cumin

2 cups vegetable stock

Garnish

2-4 handfuls spinach leaves, washed & dried

½ bunch basil, washed and dried

Preparation

Heat coconut oil and fry the onion, mustard seeds and cumin seeds until they pop. Transfer cooked onions, cumin and mustard seeds into a thick-based large casserole pot.

Add adzuki beans, tamarind water, ground spices, chillies, diced pumpkin, ground spices and stock.

Bring to the boil, reduce heat then simmer 30-35 minutes until the aduki beans and pumpkin are cooked.

Once cooked, add spinach and gently wilt, taking care while mixing not to break up the pumpkin.

Serve with spinach and lots of chopped basil.

Serves 4

There is subtle healing that occurs within when you are in the presence of a horse; energy re-balancing, and an understanding that you are in the presence of ancient wisdom, power and grace.
~ Richard Capener, Horse Whisperer

Chunky Vegetable Stew

1 medium onion, chopped

1 medium carrot, chopped

1 celery stalk, chopped

1 parsnip, chopped

¼ butternut squash, peeled and chopped

2 garlic cloves, chopped

1 medium red potato, cubed

1 tablespoon grapeseed oil

6 cups vegetable stock

2 cups diced tomatoes

¼ cup nutritional yeast

1 tablespoon Himalayan slat

¼ cup fresh or 1 teaspoon dried thyme

½ cup green peas

Preparation

Preheat oven to 350°F.

Sauté onion, carrot, celery, parsnip and squash in grape seed oil for 2-3 minutes, then add potato and sauté another couple of minutes.

Transfer sautéed vegetables to a casserole dish. Mix in stock, diced tomatoes, Himalayan salt, nutritional yeast and thyme.

Bake covered for 1-2 hours until vegetables are tender. Remove stew from oven, mix in peas and serve.

Serves 8

Curry Vegetable Stew

Vegetable puree

½ medium onion, chopped

1 small carrot, chopped

¼ butternut squash, chopped

1 small stalk celery, chopped

1 small parsnip, chopped

1 clove garlic, chopped

2 tablespoons fresh or 1 teaspoon dried thyme

1 tablespoon Himalayan salt

¼ cup nutritional yeast

½ cup tomatoes, diced

1 small red potato, chopped

1 tablespoon grape seed oil

3 cups vegetable broth or water

Stew

1 tablespoon mustard seeds

1 tablespoon coconut oil

1 small onion

1 stalk celery

1 small carrot

2 cups cooked chickpeas

1 green apple, shredded

1 tablespoon curry powder, or more to taste

1 cup almond milk

Preparation
Preheat oven to 350°F.

Vegetable puree
Add grape seed oil to a large stockpot. Sauté onion, carrot, squash, celery, parsnip and garlic until vegetables start to soften. Add curry powder, stirring for 1 minute. Add broth, potato, tomatoes, thyme, nutritional yeast and Himalayan salt. Simmer until vegetables are soft. Puree in blender until smooth.

Stew

In a skillet, toast mustard seeds in coconut oil until they pop. Add onion, celery and carrot and lightly sauté.
Pour vegetable puree into a deep baking dish. Mix in sautéed vegetables, cooked chickpeas and shredded apple. Mix in almond milk. Cover and bake for 2 hours.

Serves 8

Teriyaki Stir-Fry with Vegetable 'Un-Fried' Rice

½ onion, finely chopped

1 zucchini, finely sliced

1 carrot, finely sliced

1 celery stalk, finely sliced

½ leek, white parts only, finely chopped

½ inch piece ginger, finely diced

½ tablespoon grape seed oil

½ tablespoon tamari

½ teaspoon mirin

½ tablespoon Himalayan salt

Vegetable 'un-fried' rice

2½ cups short grain brown rice

4 cups water

½ cup onion, finely chopped

½ cup celery, finely chopped

½ cup carrot, finely chopped

½ tablespoon tamari

½ tablespoon toasted sesame oil

½ cup green peas

Preparation

Stovetop method: Place all ingredients except for peas in a saucepan and bring to a boil. Reduce temperature and simmer covered until rice is cooked, approximately 30 minutes. Add peas toward end of cooking time. Fluff with a fork.

Oven method: Preheat oven to 350° F; cook for 30 minutes then add peas. Cook for 10 more minutes. Fluff with fork.

Sauté the onion in grape seed oil until translucent. Add zucchini, carrots, celery, leek and ginger. Stir-fry 3-5 minutes until vegetables are tender crisp. Add tamari, mirin and Himalayan salt in the last minute of cooking.

Teriyaki Sauce

⅓ cup tamari

2 tablespoons

1½ tablespoons raw honey

½ cup vegetable stock

½ tablespoon arrowroot powder

Preparation

In a medium saucepan, bring tamari, mirin, honey, and vegetable stock
to a boil. Mix arrowroot powder in 3 tablespoons water and add to
sauce. Simmer until sauce starts to thicken. Yield: 1 cup
Place vegetable 'un-fried' rice on serving plate, top with stir-fried
vegetables and teriyaki sauce and serve.

Serves 4

*Walking in nature is a precious opportunity to fuel our Awareness
and experience pure WONDER once again... and again.*

~ John Parson, Nature Guide, Artist

Stuffed Sweet Red Peppers with Thyme Sauce

1 cup brown rice

½ cup white rice

2 cups water

¼ cup onion, finely chopped

¼ cup celery, finely chopped

¼ cup carrot, finely chopped

¼ cup tomato, diced

1 teaspoon Himalayan salt

1 teaspoon tamari

1 tablespoon olive oil

4 large red bell peppers

Thyme Sauce

1 cup vegetable stock

1 teaspoon tamari

1 teaspoon maple syrup

1 teaspoon thyme

1 teaspoon arrowroot powder

Preparation

Preheat oven to 350°F.

Remove center core from red peppers, keeping them whole and place them on a lightly oiled baking dish, .

In a medium saucepan, sauté onion, celery and carrot for 2-3 minutes. Add tomato, brown and white rice, Himalayan salt and tamari. Cover with water and bring to a boil. Reduce heat and simmer until rice and vegetables are tender, approximately 15 to 20 minutes.

Stuff peppers with rice mixture. Cover and bake 45 minutes.

Thyme sauce

Mix vegetable stock, tamari, maple syrup and thyme in a small saucepan and bring to a boil. Reduce heat to simmer. Mix arrowroot powder with 2 tablespoons water to dissolve. Mix into sauce and allow it to thicken. Serve stuffed peppers drizzled with thyme sauce.

Serves 4

Spinach Pasta, Roasted Vegetables and Caramelized Onions with Mixed Nut Cream Sauce

1 zucchini, julienned

1 red pepper, julienned

¼ teaspoon Himalayan salt

1 teaspoon extra virgin olive oil

Caramelized Onions

1 medium red onion, finely sliced

1 teaspoon grape seed oil

¼ teaspoon Himalayan salt

1 teaspoon balsamic vinegar

1 cup baby spinach

1 16 ounce package brown rice spinach spaghetti or fettuccini

Cream Sauce

¼ cup raw cashews

¼ cup raw almonds

2 teaspoons lemon juice

1 tablespoon paprika

1 teaspoon Dijon mustard

1 teaspoon tamari

1 tablespoon nutritional yeast

1 teaspoon Himalayan salt

Pinch pepper

Preparation

Preheat oven to 450°F. Place zucchini and red pepper on a baking sheet, coat in olive oil, and sprinkle with salt. Roast for 10 minutes.

For carmelized onions, sauté onions and salt in oil on low heat until caramelized, 5-10 minutes. Mix in balsamic vinegar.

For cream sauce, place cashews and almonds in a blender and add enough water to cover. Add remaining ingredients and blend until creamy. Set aside.

Cook pasta until 'al dente', about 10 minutes. Transfer cream sauce to a separate heatproof bowl, pull pasta from hot water and put directly into sauce and mix well. Divide spinach between individual serving dishes and top with creamed pasta., roasted vegetables and caramelized onions.

Serves 4

Zucchini Lasagna

2 zucchini, diced

1 carrot, diced

1 onion, diced

2 celery stalks, diced

½ red pepper, diced

2 garlic cloves, crushed

1 tablespoon grape seed oil

3½ cups crushed tomatoes

1 cup vegetable stock

1 tablespoon Himalayan salt

1 teaspoon agave nectar

1 bay leaf

¼ cup fresh or 1 teaspoon dried basil

1 tablespoon oregano

White sauce

2 cups almond or coconut milk

1 tablespoon brown rice flour

2 teaspoons Himalayan salt

2 teaspoons vegan spread

¼ cup vegetable stock

1 16 ounce package brown rice lasagna noodles

1 cup washed spinach leaves

Shredded vegan cheese

Preparation

Tomato Sauce

In a stockpot, sauté carrot, onion, celery, pepper and ½ tablespoon Himalayan salt in grape seed oil until vegetables are soft. Add zucchini, garlic, crushed tomatoes, vegetable stock, bay leaf, basil, oregano, ½ tablespoon Himalayan salt and agave nectar. Simmer on low heat until vegetables are tender, approximately 45 minutes.

White Sauce

Blend almond milk, brown rice flour, Himalayan salt and vegan spread in a blender on high speed. Transfer to a saucepan, add vegetable stock and simmer on low until it starts to thicken, remove from heat.

Precook brown rice lasagna (boil 4-5 minutes), remove from heat and leave in water.

Lasagna

Oil bottom and sides of a lasagna pan and layer ingredients by starting with tomato sauce, then lasagna noodles (pull them out straight from water without rinsing), white sauce, spinach leaves, lasagna noodles, tomato sauce, lasagna noodles, finishing with tomato sauce and white sauce (swirl together) and top with vegan cheese.

Preheat oven to 350°F. Cover lasagna and bake for 45 minutes. Uncover and bake for another 15 minutes. Turn off heat and let lasagna sit in warm oven until ready to serve.

Serves 8

*Blend intention with truth,
temper with patience
and be plentiful with forgiveness.
Watch synchronicities appear
and blossom into full-blown miracles.
See every new day as an
opportunity to finish life blissfully,
savouring the sweetness of what was.
Create to that end,
drifting into final timelessness,
joyfully complete.*

~ Mark Daniel, Sound Shaman

THE ADDED TOUCH
Sauces, Sides & Staples

Almond Milk

¼ cup raw almonds
2 cups water

Preparation

Blend almonds and water in blender
on high speed for 1 minute.
Strain and discard solids.

Yield: 2 cups

Coconut Milk

¼ cup shredded coconut
2 cups water

Preparation

Blend coconut and water in blender on high speed for 1 minute.
Strain and discard solids.

Yield: 2 cups

Basic Vegetable Broth

Place the peelings and skins from a variety of root vegetables (onion, celery, carrot, garlic, potato, sweet potato) in a large stock pot and cover with water.
Simmer on low until tender, 1 – 2 hours.
Strain broth and use in soups, stews or freeze in batches until needed.

Teriyaki Sauce

2/3 cup tamari
1/3 cup mirin
3 tablespoons raw honey
1 cup vegetable stock
1 tablespoon arrowroot powder

Preparation

In a medium saucepan, bring tamari, mirin, honey, and vegetable stock to a boil.
Mix arrowroot powder in ¼ cup water and add to sauce.
Simmer until sauce starts to thicken.

Yield: 2 cups

Beet and Thyme Sauce

1 cup beets, grated
4 cups vegetable stock
1 tablespoon thyme

1 teaspoon Himalayan salt
1 teaspoon tamari
1 teaspoon maple syrup

Preparation

Place grated beets, vegetable stock, thyme, salt, tamari and maple syrup in stockpot and simmer until beets are tender and liquid is reduced by half.
Place in blender on high and blend until smooth.

Yield: 2 cups

Date and Garlic Dipping Sauce

4 dates
¼ red onion, roughly chopped
2 tablespoons balsamic vinegar
1 can whole tomatoes, drained
2 garlic cloves

1 teaspoon Himalayan salt
Dash pepper
1 tablespoon Worcestershire sauce
¼ cup sundried tomatoes, soaked until soft

Preparation

Place all ingredients in a blender and blend on high speed until smooth.

Yield: 2 cups

Onions detoxify heavy metals from the body and have considerable blood-sugar lowering properties.

Balsamic Glaze

4 pears, chopped

2 cups water

1 cup balsamic vinegar

1 carrot, chopped

1 celery stalk, chopped

1 onion, chopped

1 teaspoon grape seed oil

Preparation

Cook chopped pears in water and balsamic vinegar until soft and liquid is reduced by half.

Sauté chopped carrot, celery and onion in oil until vegetables are soft.

Place sautéed vegetables and cooked pears in a blender and blend on high speed until smooth.

Yield: 1½ cups

Garlic Lovers Hemp Seed Dressing

½ cup hemp seeds

2 tablespoons olive oil

1 tablespoon Dijon mustard

½ cup lemon juice

1 tablespoon agave nectar

¼ cup apple cider vinegar

6 garlic cloves

¼ cup nutritional yeast

½ tablespoon Himalayan salt

½ teaspoon pepper

½ cup water

Preparation

Place all ingredients in a blender and process until smooth.

Yield: 2 cups

Spinach Polenta

½ cup spinach
Water to cover
1 cup cornmeal
4 cups water
½ tablespoon Himalayan salt

Preparation

Place spinach in a food processor or blender, cover with water and blend until smooth.

To make polenta, mix cornmeal with 4 cups of water and Himalayan salt in a saucepan. Add spinach and cook on low heat until mixture starts to stick to the pan. Transfer to a serving dish or cookie sheet and allow to set as polenta.

Preheat oven to 300°F. Warm polenta in oven for 15 minutes and cut into squares or wedges. Serve with tomato salsa or chutney.

Serves 4-6

Paul's Roasted Red Pepper Pasta Sauce

This recipe comes from our friends at 'The Pasta Shop' in Peterborough, Ontario, who have graciously catered many of our outdoor events.

1 can (28 ounce) plum tomatoes
3 jars roasted red peppers
1 bunch cilantro
1 handful sliced almonds
3-4 garlic cloves
Splash of red wine vinegar
Canola oil
Himalayan salt and pepper to taste
Fresh cooked pasta

Preparation

Strain tomatoes and peppers well. Remove as much liquid as possible. You may wish to strain overnight.
In a food processor, place tomatoes, peppers, cilantro, almonds and garlic. Pulse until blended. Add a splash of red wine vinegar and canola oil.
Blend until desired consistency. Season to taste.
This sauce is wonderful on fresh angel hair pasta or spaghetti.

Sesame Green Beans

2 cups green beans

¼ cup sesame seeds

2 tablespoons maple syrup

3 tablespoons apple cider vinegar

¼ cup water

Pinch Himalayan salt

½ tablespoon sesame seeds

Preparation

Blanch green beans in boiling, salted water for 2 minutes. Drain and transfer to a bowl of cold water.

For dressing, mix sesame seeds, maple syrup, apple cider vinegar, water and salt in blender until smooth. Mix in ½ tablespoon sesame seeds by hand.

Mix dressing with green beans and serve.

Serves 4

Dill and Lemon Roasted Zucchini

1 cup green zucchini, chopped

1 cup yellow zucchini, chopped

1 teaspoon dill, finely chopped

1½ tablespoons lemon juice

¼ teaspoon Himalayan salt

Dash pepper

Preparation

Preheat oven to 350°F.

Mix chopped zucchini with dill, lemon juice, salt and pepper.

Spread in roasting pan or on a cookie sheet and roast for 10-15 minutes. Shake pan half way through cooking.

Serves 4

Turmeric New Potatoes

4 cups baby potatoes, quartered
1 bay leaf, chopped
2 garlic cloves, chopped
1 tablespoon lemon juice
½ teaspoon turmeric
½ teaspoon Himalayan salt
½ tablespoon olive or grape seed oil

Preparation

Preheat oven to 375°F.
Mix quartered potatoes with bay leaf, garlic, lemon juice,
turmeric, salt and oil.
Spread on a cookie sheet and cover with parchment paper.
Roast 45 minutes until tender.

Serves 4

Look daily to be inspired
...and live daily to inspire others.

~ *Michael Marentette*

Garlic Bok Choy

1 garlic clove, finely chopped
8 baby bok choy, sliced
½ teaspoon Himalayan salt
1 teaspoon sesame oil

Preparation

Heat oil in sauté pan to medium; add garlic and sauté
for a few seconds.
Add bok choy and salt and stir-fry for 1-2 minutes, stir
in sesame oil and serve.

Serves 4

Sautéed Lemon Red Cabbage

1 small head red cabbage, thinly sliced
½ red onion, finely sliced
1 tablespoon grape seed oil
1 teaspoon Himalayan salt
Pinch pepper
2 tablespoons lemon juice

Preparation

Sauté cabbage and onion in skillet in grape seed oil and Himalayan
salt until cabbage is tender.
Season with pepper and mix in lemon juice.

Serves 4

A healthy life is about creating opportunities and exploring them to taste the sweetness within each. There is always something new to experience, to learn, an opportunity to grow ... a chance encounter, a random act of kindness, all can have a profound impact on you. Self-awareness, gratitude, taking in and giving out - this is a recipe for a continuous stream of health and vitality.

~ Alison Cohen, Consultant & Life Adventurer

FIT AND FUN

Healthy Snacks for Everyone

Janet's Healthy Watermelon Freeze Pops

3 cups seedless watermelon, chopped

½ cup fresh blueberries

½ cup chopped fresh strawberries

1 kiwi, peeled and sliced

1 peach or nectarine, diced

A handful of fresh cherries, pitted and chopped

Preparation

Purée the watermelon in a blender until smooth; set aside.

Fill freeze pop molds with the chopped fresh fruit and then pour in the watermelon puree until each mold is full to the top.

Insert the cap into each filled mold.

Place in freezer 2-3 hours.

Organically grown watermelon is one of the worlds healthiest foods when left to ripen before eating. Recent studies show that it is an excellent resource for cardio vascular health, reducing weight and inflammation. Watermelon is rich with Vitamin C and it contains antioxidants.

Healthy Popcorn

1 cup organic corn, popped

Preparation

Toss popped corn with one of the variations below:

Variations

½ teaspoon Himalayan salt and 2 tablespoons of oil (either extra virgin olive oil, pumpkin seed oil or flax seed oil)

½ teaspoon Bragg Organic Sprinkle Seasoning

1 teaspoon ground dulse

1 teaspoon gomashio

1 tablespoon nutritional yeast

To make gomashio toast 5 tablespoons of sesame seeds in a 350°F oven until they start to brown, approximately 4 to 6 minutes. Cool and blend together with 1 tablespoon of Himalayan salt. Also great on salads, or added to soup.

Tomoko's Oh-So-Green Pea and Avocado Guacamole

1¾ cups green peas, cooked

2 garlic cloves, finely chopped

2 tablespoons lemon juice

2 tablespoons cilantro

1 avocado

¼ cup tomatoes

1 teaspoon Himalayan salt

Pinch pepper

Preparation

Coarsely chop green peas in a food processor. Add garlic, lemon juice cilantro, Himalayan salt and a pinch of pepper to combine.

Peel avocados and coarsely chop. Seed and coarsely chop tomatoes.

Mix avocados and tomatoes into the green pea mixture.

Yield: 2½ cups

Apricot Cilantro Salsa

1 cup dried apricots, chopped

2 tablespoons agave nectar

3 tablespoons apple cider vinegar

1 tablespoon cilantro, chopped

1 teaspoon curry powder

Dash of chili flakes, optional

Preparation

Cover chopped apricots with water and soak for at least 15
minutes and drain.

Blend remainder of ingredients, except the chili flakes, in blender.

Pour dressing over soaked apricots and marinate for 15-30
minutes before serving.

Sprinkle with chili flakes, if desired.

Yield: 1½ cups

Homemade Kale Chips

1 bunch fresh organic kale

¼ cup extra virgin olive oil

2 garlic cloves, minced

Juice of half a lemon

Himalayan salt (to taste)

Pinch of cumin (to taste)

Preparation

Preheat oven to 300°F . Wash kale and cut it into 2-3 inch long strips. Put
the kale in a large bowl and toss with olive oil, Himalayan salt, diced garlic,
lemon juice, and cumin.

Allow the kale to marinade for 20 minutes. Spread the kale on a baking
tray. Bake for 30 minutes, rotating the pan and stirring after 15 minutes.

When you are faced with obstacles, persist until you find a way to get over, through, or around them. Persist when you face challenges and adversity. Enlist trusted friends who will support you through your journey. Be determined to achieve your dreams no matter what. Persistence takes willpower, the constant ingredient summoned by those who know success.

~ Lori Raudnask, Inspirational Coach and Trainer

NIGHTLY REWARDS

Desserts for a Sweet Life

Date Stuffed Baked Apples

2 apples (Gala or Granny Smith)
4 dates
3 teaspoons maple syrup
8 toasted walnuts, chopped
Dash of cinnamon

Preparation

Mix chopped walnuts with 1 teaspoon maple syrup; lightly toast in a
skillet until golden.
Cut off each end of apple and core.
Stuff with dates and pour 2 teaspoons maple syrup on top.
Preheat oven to 350°F. Bake apples in a shallow baking dish until tender
– approximately 30 minutes for Gala and 15 minutes for granny Smith.
Serve with toasted walnuts and a sprinkle of cinnamon.

Serves 2

Mixed Nuts and Chocolate Tofu Ice Cream

½ cup raw cashews

½ cup raw almonds (slivered, no skin)

Water to cover

¼ cup maple syrup

½ cup cocoa powder

1 package silken tofu

Preparation

Mix cashews, almonds, water, maple syrup and cocoa powder in a blender. Add tofu and process until smooth.

Place in a shallow pan, cover with plastic and freeze until needed. To serve, scoop out into pretty ice cream dishes.

Serves 10

Brown Rice with Apricots, Pomegranates and Raspberry Cream

½ cup cooked brown rice

3 tablespoons nuts and seeds (pumpkin seeds, almonds and cashews)

4 dried apricots, coarsely chopped

Rind of half a small orange

Rind or half a small lemon

1 pomegranate

Preparation

Soak nuts and seeds in plenty of water overnight. Soak apricots with just enough water to cover overnight. In the morning, drain and rinse the nuts; drain the apricots and retain the soaking juice.

Remove the seeds from the pomegranate, discarding all the bitter white pith. Mix all ingredients in a bowl, with half the apricot soaking juice. Serve in a bowl with a dollop of raspberry cream.

Raspberry Cream

¼ cup frozen or fresh raspberries

½ large ripe banana

½ ripe avocado

Pinch Himalayan salt

Half the apricot soaking juice

Preparation

Blend all ingredients until smooth.

Pour onto cooked brown rice and enjoy.

Serves 1

Sunflower Seed Cocoa Balls

1 cup raw sunflower seeds
½ cup shredded coconut + 3 tablespoons
2 tablespoons maple syrup or 1 tablespoon agave nectar
¾ cup sultana raisins
1 tablespoon cocoa powder

Preparation

In a blender, pulse sunflower seeds, shredded coconut, maple syrup, raisins and cocoa powder until combined.

With your hands, form the mixture into 2" balls and then roll them in the additional shredded coconut.

Place on a cookie sheet so they do not touch and freeze at least 1 hour. Remove from freezer 1 hour before serving.

Makes approximately 1 dozen

Sweet Potato Pie

5 cups sweet potatoes, peeled and diced
½ cup maple syrup
2 teaspoons cinnamon
1 teaspoon nutmeg
5 eggs

Pie Crust

1 cup brown rice flour
¼ cup raw sugar
¼ cup olive oil
1 egg
2 teaspoons coconut or almond milk (if crust too thick)

Preparation

Steam diced sweet potatoes until soft. Cool.
Place cooled sweet potatoes, maple syrup, cinnamon, nutmeg and eggs in a food processor. Blend until smooth.

Crust

Preheat oven to 300°F.
Place brown rice flour, sugar, olive oil and egg in food processor. Pulse until combined. Thin with coconut or almond milk if mixture is too thick. Press into bottom of 10" pie plate.
Pour sweet potato mixture onto crust and bake 30-45 minutes until set. Top will have a custard texture. Do not overcook.
Cool and serve with sprinkled with cinnamon.

Serves 8

Chocolate Banana and Avocado Pudding

2 dates, roughly chopped
1 avocado
1 banana, very ripe and frozen
¼ cup raw cacao powder
2 tablespoons maple syrup
Chopped fresh banana, fresh berries, mint for serving

Preparation

Place dates in food processor, pulse, then add frozen banana, then avocado. Mix until combined.
Transfer mixture to a blender and add cacao powder and maple syrup. Blend on high speed until smooth.
Divide into serving dishes and serve with chopped fresh bananas, fresh berries and mint

Serves 4

Very Mixed Berry Almond and Cashew Cream Cake

Crust

½ cup brown rice flour

2 tablespoons raw sugar

2 tablespoons raw cocoa

2 tablespoons olive oil

1 egg

1 teaspoon coconut or almond milk (to thin if crust is too thick)

Topping

½ cup raw cashews

½ cup raw slivered almonds

Water to cover

½ cup fresh mixed berries

¼ cup lemon juice

1 tablespoon agave nectar

Preparation

To prepare crust, place brown rice flour, sugar, cocoa, olive oil and egg in a food processor and pulse until combined. If dough is to thick, thin out with coconut or almond milk. Press into bottom of pie plate or spring form pan.

To prepare topping, place cashews and almonds in blender and add enough water to cover. Add lemon juice and agave nectar. Blend until smooth. Pour over prepared crust and freeze at least 1 hour.

Serves 6

Fresh Ginger Banana Bread

2 cups rice flour

½ cup raw sugar

¼ cup maple syrup

¾ teaspoon Himalayan salt

1 tablespoon fresh ginger, finely minced

¾ teaspoon cinnamon

¾ teaspoon nutmeg

½ cup water

1 teaspoon apple cider vinegar

2 cups mashed bananas

¼ cup grape seed oil

1 teaspoon vanilla

½ cup chopped walnuts for topping

Preparation

Preheat oven to 350°F. Lightly oil a 5" x 9" loaf pan and set aside.

In a medium mixing bowl, sift together flour, sugar, baking soda, salt, fresh ginger, cinnamon and nutmeg.

In a large mixing bowl, whisk together water and apple cider vinegar and let stand for 2 minutes. Add the mashed bananas, oil, maple syrup and vanilla extract. Whisk together until well combined.

Fold dry ingredients into the wet ingredients. Do not over mix. Fold in walnuts and pour batter into prepared loaf pan.

Bake 1 hour, or until toothpick inserted into middle, comes out clean.

Allow bread to cool on a wire rack for 20 minutes.

Yield: 1 loaf

Oh to the joy of chocolate
a ceremony of soulful delight...

Chocolate Fudge Cake with Mesquite, Banana and Chocolate Mousse

½ cup shredded coconut

¼ cup raw almonds

Water to cover

¼ cup raw cocoa powder

¼ cup cocoa nibs

¼ cup carob chips

½ teaspoon almond essence

2 eggs

¼ cup raw mesquite powder

Mousse

3 large soft bananas

¼ cup maple syrup

½ cup mesquite powder

Preparation

Preheat oven to 300°F.

Place shredded coconut and almonds in blender. Cover with water and blend on high speed for one minute. Drain excess milk through a sieve and return the dry part into the blender.

Add cocoa powder, cocoa nibs, carob chips, almond essence, eggs and mesquite and blend for another minute.

Pour into a 9" x 12" parchment-lined pan and bake for 30 minutes or until set. Cool.

To prepare mousse, blend bananas, maple syrup and mesquite powder on high speed until smooth.

Frost top of cake with mousse and decorate as desired.

Serves 10

Celebration Carrot Cake with Nut Cream Icing

1 cup brown rice flour

1 teaspoon baking powder

½ teaspoon baking soda

2 eggs

¼ cup raw sugar

1 tablespoon maple syrup

3 cups carrots, shredded

¼ cup coconut oil

1 teaspoon cinnamon

Nut Cream Icing

1 cup raw cashews

1 cup raw almonds

Water to cover

¼ cup lemon juice

¼ cup agave nectar

Preparation

Preheat oven to 350°F.

In a mixing bowl, cream eggs, sugar and maple syrup until light and fluffy.

Mix together flour, baking powder, baking soda and cinnamon. Add to cream mixture, along with carrots and coconut oil. Blend until well combined. If mixture is too thick, thin out with a little almond milk or water. Pour into an oiled and floured 9" x 12" baking pan. Bake 20-30 minutes or until toothpick comes out clean. Cool.

To prepare icing, place cashews and almonds in a blender and cover with water. Add lemon juice and agave and blend on high speed until smooth and creamy.

Spread icing on top and sides of cooled carrot cake and decorate as desired.

Serves 10

Buddha Balls

2 cups plain almonds, finely ground
½ cup carob powder or cocoa
⅓ teaspoon Himalayan salt

1 cup shredded coconut
¾ cup agave or brown rice syrup
2 tablespoons olive oil

As an option you can also add a handful of additional ingredients, such
as ground pumpkin seeds, hemp seeds, raisins or currants.

Preparation

Mix almonds, carob powder, Himalayan salt, shredded coconut, agave
nectar, olive oil and your choice of ingredients. With your hands, form
mixture into 2" balls. Roll them in shredded coconut, or cocoa powder
or leave plain. Can be served immediately or they will keep in the
fridge for several days.

*Ah-h-h Life - Hail to sweet
glorious Earth...
Within the ancient art
of Geomancy, mankind
came to understand how
the mineral kingdom is
behind all life forms, how
geology contributed to the
evolution of the planet; the
very grains within your
bones. So dear people walk
gently upon the earth -
for she is alive and
pulsating into tomorrow.*

~ Nala, Druid

Chocolate Truffles

1½ cups raw cashews

3 dozen organic dates

½ an organic lemon

½ teaspoon vanilla extract

½ pound of high quality organic fair trade dark chocolate, or 1 package of dark chocolate vegan baking chips.

Preparation

Place dates in a small saucepan and add enough spring water to cover bottom of pan. Bring to a boil and simmer while stirring until dates soften and a thick "date jam" is formed. Turn off heat and allow dates to cool.

Blend cashews, juice of lemon, dates and vanilla extract in a food processor.

Place in a bowl in the freezer and allow to harden for an hour or overnight.

In a double boiler, melt the dark chocolate to liquid. Keep the heat on minimum once it's melted, and work quickly. Using a melon-baller or a small round spoon, scoop out the cashew-date mixture and drop into a larger round spoon.

Ladle melted chocolate over the ball, covering it entirely. Place truffles on a cookie sheet lined with parchment paper.

Put the cookie sheet in the fridge to allow the chocolate to set.

Arrange beautifully on a plate and sprinkle with organic cocoa powder.

Yield: Approximately 3 dozen

Raw Chocolate Chili Truffles

¾ cup coconut oil
¾ cup agave nectar
½ cup cocoa powder
1 teaspoon Himalayan salt
½ teaspoon pure vanilla extract
Dash of cayenne or chili pepper

Preparation

In a food processor mix all ingredients except coconut oil. Melt the coconut oil on a stove top or in a bowl of hot water. Once melted, add to the ingredients in the food processor and blend until smooth.
Pour chocolate into a piping bag or a plastic bag with the corner snipped off. Pipe out a line about an inch thick onto a nonstick surface (parchment paper works great or a non-stick baking sheet). Place into the freezer to harden. Once they are solid, cut into desired sizes.
Be careful about handling them, as they are very heat sensitive.
Sprinkle with Himalayan salt for a surprising taste sensation! Enjoy!

Raw Apple Pie

2½ cups almonds, finely ground

1 cup pitted medjool dates

¼ teaspoon Himalayan salt

2 medium apples, peeled, cored and chopped

2 medium apples, cored and thinly sliced (to fold into mixture)

1 tablespoon fresh lemon juice

1 tablespoon fresh lemon juice for sliced apples

½ cup pitted soaked Medjool dates

½ cup soaked raisins

¼ teaspoon ground cinnamon

1 teaspoon coconut oil

2 tablespoons maple syrup

Preparation

Crust

Process the dates and almonds in food processor until they resemble crumbs. Be careful not to over process otherwise the nuts will become too oily.

Place the mixture into a 9-inch tart pan (with removable bottom); distribute the crumbs evenly along the bottom of the pan and up the sides. Start pressing it in tightly along the sides to form a pie shell. Place in freezer for 15 minutes.

Pie

In a food processor, combine the 2 chopped apples, soaked and
drained raisins and the dates. Add the cinnamon, lemon juice,
maple syrup and coconut butter. Process until very smooth.
Place the 2 thinly sliced apples in a large bowl and sprinkle the with
lemon juice; add the mixture from the food processor, stirring in
gently so as not to break up the sliced apples.
Remove crust from the freezer; pour the apple filling into the crust.
Press it down gently with a spatula and place in the refrigerator
for a couple of hours to set. Covered with plastic wrap, the pie will
keep in the refrigerator for up to 3 days.
When ready to serve, top with a spoonful of cashew cream
on page 57.

Serves: 6

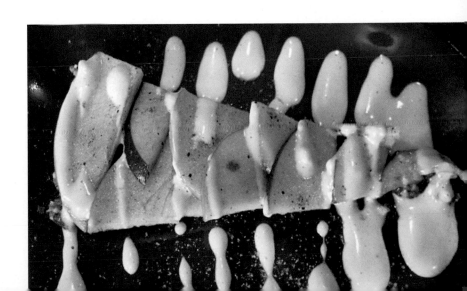

Do things on the spur of the moment...
when inspiration strikes, when the energy is right.
This is when the magic happens
and gives us the joy of surprise to our life.

~ Annie Thompson, Designer

Tofu Chocolate Torte

Filling

1 package silken tofu

¼ cup soy milk

¼ cup packed pitted dates

⅓ cup organic cocoa powder

2 tablespoons melted coconut oil

1 teaspoon pure vanilla extract

½ teaspoon orange zest

Crust

½ cup unsweetened flaked coconut

½ cup ground raw almonds

¾ cup spelt flour

1 teaspoon fresh ground nutmeg

2 tablespoons coconut oil

¼ cup pitted dates

Preparation

For the crust, blend the almonds and dates in a food processor, then add the rest of the ingredients and knead until it forms a ball. Press into a 9" round pan and chill.

For the filling, blend all ingredients in a food processor until smooth and pour into the chilled crust and refrigerate until firm. Garnish with mint leaf and any red berries to serve.

Serves 8

Carob Nut Log

1 cup raw almonds

2 cups raw sunflower seeds

1 cup organic raisins

1 cup raw walnuts

1 cup raw carob powder

Shredded coconut for garnishing

Chopped nuts (optional)

Preparation

Cover almonds, sunflower seeds, and raisins with water and soak
1 hour. Reserve 2 tablespoons soaking liquid. Drain the almonds,
sunflower seeds and raisens. Place in food processor with the soaking
liquid and process until smooth. Add the rest of the ingredients.
Adjust the sweetness to your liking as you add the raw carob powder.
Once the whole thing is smooth, roll the mixture on a flat surface so it
binds to form a log.
Frost it with the Avocado Frosting. Garnish with shredded coconut.

Avocado Frosting

1 cup golden raisins, soaked

1 cup water for soaking

1 ripe avocado

3 tablespoons organic maple syrup

1 teaspoon pure vanilla extract

½ cup raw carob powder

Preparation

Soak the green raisins in the water for an hour. Pour the water and raisins into your food processor; blend the avocado and maple syrup together.

Gradually add the vanilla extract and then the carob powder. You'll need to adjust the sweetness to your liking as you add the raw carob powder.

Once thoroughly blended, use it to frost the Carob Nut Log. Sprinkle with shredded coconut.

Garnish with orange zest peel and mint leaf.

Serves 2

Chia, Banana and Coconut Ice Cream Pie

1 cup shredded coconut

1 cup water

4 dates

2 cups chia pudding

4 frozen bananas

Shredded coconut for topping

Chia Pudding

1 cup vanilla-flavored unsweetened almond milk

1 cup plain low-fat Greek style yogurt

2 tablespoons maple syrup, plus more for serving

1 teaspoon vanilla extract

Kosher salt

1/4 cup chia seeds

Preparation

In a medium bowl, gently whisk the almond milk, yogurt, maple syrup, vanilla and a pinch of salt until just blended. Whisk in the chia seeds; let stand 30 minutes. Stir to distribute the seeds if they have settled. Cover and refrigerate overnight. Yield: 2 cups

Preparation

Crust

Preheat oven to 350°F. Place shredded coconut, water and dates in food processor and pulse until combined. Press into bottom of pie plate and bake for 15 minutes or until sides begin to brown. Cool. Break frozen bananas into chunks. Place chia pudding and frozen bananas in food processor and blend until smooth. Pour into baked pie shell, sprinkle with shredded coconut and freeze.

Serves 8

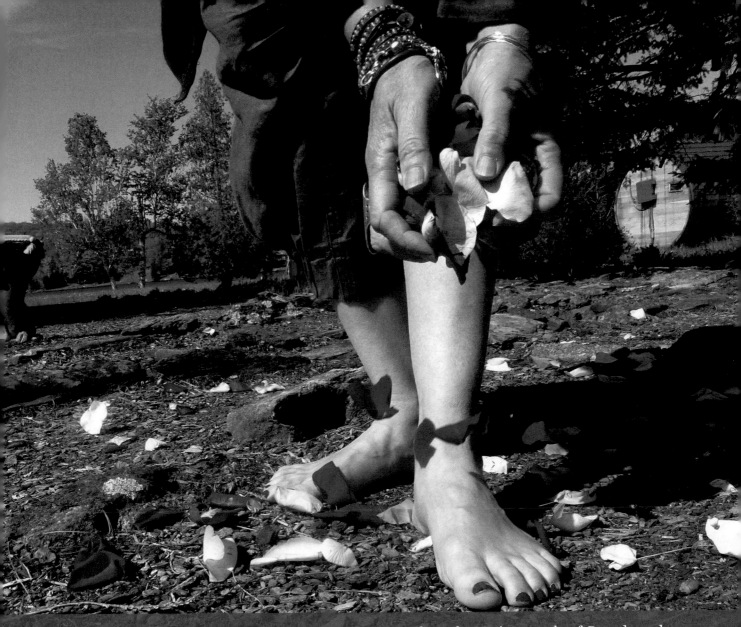

The following beautiful words of thanksgiving come to us from the Native people of Canada and upstate New York, known as the Iroquois or Six Nations People, who walked and cared for this land.

Sakarihwahó:ton - Closing Words
We have now arrived at the place where we end our words.
Of all the things we have named, it was not our intention to leave anything out.
If something was forgotten, we leave it to each individual
to send greetings and thanks in their own way.
Éhtho niiohtónha'k ne onkwa'nikón:ra ~ And now our minds are One.

*A Maze is meant
to get you Lost*

*A Labyrinth is meant
to get you Found*

*Grail Springs is that
Labyrinth*

About Grail Springs Retreat ~ a Centre for Personal Transformation since 2001

Grail Springs thrives on its mission to heal people, animals and planet. The programs are based on a complete, holistic philosophy by its creator Madeleine Marentette. In her quest, which began in the late 80's for her own personal healing and spiritual enlightenment, Madeleine has developed 'The 7 Essentials of Life' that address the inter-relatedness of our entire being. Grail Springs and its programs are the embodiment of her endeavors to bring awareness to the four bodies of self; physical, mental, emotional and spiritual. Through a series of weekly talks, workshops and life-transforming events, individuals are not only immersed in the experience of self-care but also in self-development, and are inspired to take the necessary steps to change their life in so many ways for the better ~ body, mind and soul.

Grail Springs is located in Bancroft, Ontario, the 'Mineral Capital of Canada', rich in quartz, marble, sodalite and hundreds of other minerals. Grounded in potent healing attributes from these unique mineral deposits of the land, the healthy forests, abundant wildlife, and the alkaline waters of the lake, Grail Springs serves as the perfect healing vessel for seekers of health and wellness. This unique environment supports the foundation of the seven aspects of the program which include; assessment, detoxification, nutrition, breath work, yoga, meditation and support. The programs at Grail Springs are delivered by a caring team of dedicated staff, healers, nutritionists and professional coaches.

From the very beginning, Grail Springs adopted the pH balanced approach to diet otherwise known as 'The Alkaline Diet', now recognized by naturopaths and doctors alike as one of the most important revelations to assure optimum health. An alkaline-based food plan that is integrated into a lifetime plan will help to reverse years of dietary neglect and will effectively support our body at the deepest core, ensuring a happy, healthy and long life.

This book was designed to assist readers and the guests of Grail Springs to live healthy and beautiful lives.

For more information about Grail Springs Retreat Centre for Wellbeing go to: www.grailsprings.com

Testimonials From our Guests

Dear Madeleine, I just wanted to send you a heartfelt 'Thank you' for all you have created and brought into this world through the power of your being... God bless. ~ Birgit A.

The Grail is one of my most favorite places to be in the world. The land is truly magical. ~ Tara G.

Grail Springs Retreat is beyond words. It's like a bath for the soul! ~Bari M.

Thank you for your kindness, generosity, wisdom and guidance. Every moment spent with you and Grail Springs is a gift. ~Susan E.

Grail Springs is like the home for our souls! ~Vere L.

You have truly created a magical sanctuary for rejuvenation and healing. The staff went above and beyond. ~S. B.

Thank you for sharing your gifts of care, smiles and light with me this week. With gratitude and reverence, a beautiful space to restore and reconnect with yourself. Wonderful hospitality. Caring 'Soul Food"! ~ Susan Y.

I hoped for the full experience, and was given the full experience. Madeleine's creation is concrete and palpable. Grail itself is a wonderful nesting space; quality, comfort and imagination infuse the building. ~ Diana E.

A must on your list for an amazing retreat. I highly recommend it. And feel the spirit of the land! ~Kimberly M.

This place is my heaven on earth. Absolutely beautiful :) Thanks to all who make me well while I'm there so that I can go back and live in the world. ~Tracey R.

Spent a week at Grail that will never be forgotten. My life is forever changed and blessed. Namaste ~Amanda T.

Healing happens so deeply here...my heart filled with offerings of gratitude, humility, grace and reverence. ~Allie M.

Thank you so very much for the fabulous time. Everyone was so gracious, friendly and helpful. It was such a pleasure sharing time and space with all of you. I wish all of you much peace, joy, laughter and abundance in all you do. With great appreciation and gratitude. ~ Kathy C.

Madeleine, I would like to thank you for sharing your experiences and knowledge... You are truly a gifted teacher, I feel blessed to have been able to participate... Bless you. ~ Kathy B.

Thank you for creating such a wonderful sanctuary! I have loved being here and can feel the magic that is present! ~ Y. E.

I keep running out of superlatives. I can only put hand over heart, look heavenward and give thanks! ~Lucille N.

What you have created at Grail Springs is so special and meaningful to so many people because of what it does for the soul by nurturing and healing. ~Linda B.

Thank you from the bottom of my heart. You have INSPIRED me deeply and you have TRANSFORMED my life... BLESS all of you. ~ Shirley R.

From the moment I arrived, I knew that this was going to be a very special week... Every aspect of this wellness spa is perfect... The quality of the food, treatments and accommodations is out of this world. For me it was the culmination of a very long journey, which now has a more defined purpose and path. Thank you. ~Elaine B.

I came to Grail Springs for rest and relaxation, but what I received in addition was a transformative spiritual experience... I leave this wonderful place feeling much more centred in my strength of being - and utterly grateful. ~Felicitas R.

My trip to Grail Springs has been the best thing I have ever done for myself. ~Natalie F.

I've been to many sacred places all over the world and Grail Springs in up there as #1. Thank you all for all you do. ~S. Wolf.

Dearest Madeleine, our stay at Grail Springs was utterly transformative. Our personal consultations with you were life changing. I felt like I was knighted! Please accept our deepest gratitude for all that transpired and the opportunity to participate in the experience that is Grail Springs... ~ Manny J. & Celeste S.

The Grail is the most beautiful, restorative place on Earth! ~ Michele M.

Madeleine, I can't believe my good fortune at having found you and Grail Springs, which have added such luster and light to my life!... I truly feel transformed, and that is no small accomplishment!! Thank you for helping me to find my spiritual home! ~ Bonnie T.

One of the most beautiful sacred sites I have ever played at. ~ Debbie D.

When I decided that I needed a place to go to detox and cleanse, I had no idea that I would find a place like the Grail... I came out with so much more and that was the spiritual healing, which I was not expecting... Thank you to Madeleine and all the staff for this special gift that will keep on giving. ~Debbie K.

There is something special about Madeleine's presence, her way of being, and her way of communicating. When Madeleine speaks to you, you feel something deep inside of you ignite. The information she conveys enters you at a very deep level, and you are forever changed for your highest good. ~Michele C.

My experience and growth was life changing. I am so blessed to know you and this sacred place. It feels like I am in Heaven. My heart is forever enlightened and blossoming. Thank YOU!!! ~Jacolyn J.

Glossary

Many of the ingredients for in *Recipes for Life: Beautiful Food and Words to Live By* may not be familiar. Below is a list of ingredients with a brief description. Most ingredients listed will be found at your local health food store, or may be ordered on-line.

Acai Berry Powder
Acai berries are native to the rainforests of South America. They are considered to aid in many health concerns, including arthritis, weight loss, high cholesterol, healthy skin and detoxification.

Adzuki beans
Adzuki beans are a good source for Iron, magnesium, potassium, zinc and folic acid.

Agave nectar
Agave nectar is a sugar substitute, derived from the agave plant found in South and Central America.

Arame seaweed
Arame is high in calcium, iodine, iron, magnesium, and vitamin A.
Arrowroot powder
Arrowroot powder a root starch that acts as a thickener just as cornstarch.

Ashwagandha powder
Ashwagandha supports the immune system and liver function

Bragg Organic Sprinkle Seasoning
A blend of herbs and spices used to add flavor. (Gluten free.)

Buckwheat (flour/groats)
Buckwheat is a fruit seed that is related to rhubarb and sorrel making it a good substitute for grains.

Cacao nibs
Cacao nibs have a chocolate flavor. They are source of antioxidants, vitamins, minerals and fiber.

Camu camu berry powder
Fruit from a shrub found in rain forests of Brazil and Peru, with vitamin C, calcium, iron, beta-carotene, niacin, thiamin and protein.

Carob powder
Rich with vitamin A, B vitamins, and several minerals, carob can replace chocolate or cocoa in recipes

Chia seeds/chia seed powder
Chia seeds are a source of omega-3 fatty acids, anti-oxidants, minerals, vitamins and dietary fiber.

Chlorella powder
Green unicellular freshwater algae that is rich in protein, vitamins (including vitamin B12), minerals (especially iron), amino and nucleic acids.

Five-spice powder
A mixture of spices used especially in Chinese cooking, usually including cinnamon, cloves, fennel seed, pepper, and star anise.

Flax seeds/flax seed powder
Flaxseeds are a rich source of micronutrients, dietary fiber, manganese, vitamin B1, and omega-3.

Goji berries
Goji berries grow shrubs in China, Mongolia and in the Tibetan Himalayas. Used in traditional Chinese medicine. Goji berries are rich in antioxidants.

Gomashio
Gomashio is often used as a salt replacement.

Grapeseed oil
Grape seed oil is high in polyunsaturated fats and Vitamin E,

Hemp seeds
Hemp seeds contain polyunsaturated fatty acids believed to be beneficial in reducing hypertension, cardiovascular disease, diabetes, arthritis and cancer.

Himalayan salt
Pink in colour, Himalayan salt is rich with trace minerals and electrolytes. It is used as a healthier alternative to regular salt.

Jicama
Jícama is high in carbohydrates in the form of dietary fiber. It contains protein and lipids

Kefir
Kefir contains minerals, vitamins, and essential amino acids.

Liquid smoke
Liquid smoke is a liquid seasoning used to add a smoky flavour to various foods.

Maca X-6 powder
Maca is a root from Peru. Maca contains calcium, magnesium, phosphorus, essential vitamins and minerals as well as antioxidants.

Maqui powder
Maqui is a source of Vitamin C and antioxidants.

Mirin
Sweet cooking rice wine

Mung beans
Mung beans are a source of protein, thiamin, niacin, vitamin B6, iron, magnesium, phosphorus and potassium. They are a good source of dietary fiber, vitamins C and K, riboflavin, folate and copper.

Nori sheets
Traditionally used for sushi, nori sheets are rich in vitamins E, K, A, C and B6. They are a good source of protein.

Nutritional yeast
Nutritional yeast does not froth like baking yeast. It contains B-vitamins, folic acid, selenium, zinc, and protein.

Quinoa
Quinoa is a wheat free alternative to starchy grains.

Sesame oil
Sesame oil is an antioxidant, and is beneficial to skin.

Umeboshi plum
Japanese style traditional pickle believed to be good for digestion, prevention of nausea, and for systemic toxicity,

Spirulina powder
Blue-green freshwater algae packed with fibre, protein, vitamins (A, B1, B2, B6 and K), essential minerals (iron, calcium and magnesium), trace minerals, essential fatty acids, and antioxidants.

Stevia
Stevia is a sweetener and sugar substitute.

Super greens powder
There are numerous brands available. The ingredient s often include: vegetables and grains (wheatgrass, spinach, broccoli, aquatic plants and algae (kelp, spirulina, chlorella), probiotics and enzymes.

Tamari
Tamari is a type of soy sauce.

Wakame seaweed
Wakame is edible seaweed rich in magnesium, iodine, calcium, iron and Vitamins A, C, E and K.

Acknowledgements

I will have life-long fondness and gratitude for the love and creativity of Chef Tomoko Kominami. Chef Tomoko has been teaching and sharing her passion and talent with so many thousands of guests who have stayed at Grail Springs Retreat Centre for Wellbeing. She may never fully realize how many people she has helped over the years with her healing food, inspiring so many individuals to make change in their lives for their own benefit, and for the benefit of their loved ones

A special thank you to the positively joyful Yvette Krotky who painstakingly scribed and tested each one of Chef Tomoko's beautiful creations with focused dedication. To Marsha Pace, our desktop publisher and graphic designer, also my friend and colleague for over 35 years, who worked with me day-in and day-out until we got ridiculously giddy and ate far too much dark chocolate. Marsha has presented my vision of beauty and life in this book with ease and much joy. To Claire Lesage, our energetic and creative editor who walked into our life at the right place at the right time. You just can't edit those great moments in life!

To my creative artists and photographer friends who contributed beautiful photos captured over the years, archiving so many special moments that have taken place at Grail Springs. Choosing photos for the book was a challenge as we poured over thousands of images bringing back so many special memories.. I thank all of my friends who generously donated their beautiful food recipes and words of wisdom with an open heart, sharing their love for community, and their purpose for walking in this world. A special acknowledgement to the dedicated staff who uphold the vessel we call Grail Springs, for they take what is, and fill the cup with plenty. And finally, to the entire Grail Springs community; loyal guests, staff, family and friends, horses and animal companions, colleagues, speakers and change-makers of the world... Grail Springs exists because of you.

We are all in this together.

~ my love and appreciation, Madeleine Marentette

We at Grail Springs give thanks to our Chalice Lake ~

Water that fills our healing vessels to assist others every day.

Thank you to all the Waters of the world.

You are life.

You quench our thirst, give us food,

Cleanse our body and our Earth.

You provide us with both strength and solace.

We know your powers and your mysteries in many forms ~

Waterfalls and streams, early morning mists and oceans wide

And in our tears of love, liquid pearls of the heart

~ We give thanks

Recipe Index

Find a Beautiful Place
And Get Lost....